UNLIKELY GRACE

THIS IS MY STORY, THIS IS MY SONG: REFLECTIONS, REVELATIONS & HONEST QUESTIONS FOR *THE CHURCH* I LOVE.

Denise Chaney

Unlikely Grace

©2021 Denise Chaney. All rights reserved.

No part of this book may be reproduced or transmitted in any form, or by any means, electronic or mechanical, included photocopying, recording or by any information storage or retrieval system, without express written permission from Denise Chaney.

Unless otherwise indicated, all Scripture quotations are taken from the Holy Bible, New Living Translation, copyright © 1996, 2004, 2015 by Tyndale House Foundation. Used by permission of Tyndale House Publishers, Carol Stream, Illinois 60188. All rights reserved.

Scripture quotations marked (NIV) are taken from the Holy Bible, New International Version®, NIV®. Copyright © 1973, 1978, 1984, 2011 by Biblica, Inc.™ Used by permission of Zondervan. All rights reserved worldwide. www.zondervan.com The "NIV" and "New International Version" are trademarks registered in the United States Patent and Trademark Office by Biblica, Inc.™

Scripture quotations marked NKJV are taken from the New King James Version®. Copyright © 1982 by Thomas Nelson. Used by permission. All rights reserved.

Scripture quotations marked TPT are from The Passion Translation®. Copyright © 2017, 2018 by Passion & Fire Ministries, Inc. Used by permission. All rights reserved. ThePassionTranslation.com.

Scripture quotations marked MSG are taken from THE MESSAGE, copyright © 1993, 2002, 2018 by Eugene H. Peterson. Used by permission of NavPress, represented by Tyndale House Publishers. All rights reserved.

ISBN: 978-1-7354852-5-6

Published by:
NarratusCreative | NarratusPress
P.O. Box 1413
Hamilton, OH 45012

Design: NarratusCreative | narratuscreative.com
Front Cover Photo Credit: Prixel Creative
Silverware Cross Photo Credit: Prixel Creative
Back Cover Photo Credit: Scott Richie

Produced in the United States of America

unlikelygrace.com | denisechaney.com

DEDICATION

This book is dedicated to my family—immediate and extended, by blood and by Holy Spirit. We are *The Church*.

I love us—warts and all.

Acknowledgments & Grateful Thanks

There is no way that a book like this could possibly cover all of the truth the Lord reveals in one life or the depth of those revelations. His Word is filled with layers and layers of goodness just waiting for our discovery. I ask you, dear reader, to prayerfully read and receive what He is saying to you.

He's such a personal God. He meets us where we are and if we allow Him, teaches us everything we need to know. I am so grateful to Him for daily grace and mercy. His love is the most compelling love I've ever known. His blood covers my multitude of disgraces. He is mine and I am His.

I have had the prayerful counsel of many advisors through writing, through processing my story and how it relates to *The Church*. I can never thank each of them enough, but I want you, the reader, to understand how much teamwork has gone into getting this book done.

To those people who were The Church *and showed me Jesus: I wouldn't be writing my story if you hadn't obeyed the Lord. Many of your names lie within these pages and you have graciously allowed me share pieces of our story. Many more people are not named here but have impacted my life profoundly. My love for each of you is immense and my heart is filled with gratitude.*

To my friends & family who agreed to share a part of their story: I am forever grateful for you all and your beautiful story(s), still unfolding. I love you and I am proud to call you my people.

To my husband, David, my knight-in-shining-civic, my closest ally and love: You've been with me from the start, encouraging me every step of the way. We've spent countless hours reading over pages, working out rough drafts and reflecting on the goodness of God in our lives. You are as much a part of this work as me. And though I didn't change all of the sentences that started with preposition :) I am forever grateful to you, Babes. I love you with all of my heart.

To our children, Devin and Ashley, who are a part of my heart and a part of the reason for every story I share: I'm so grateful you are our children. Through the writing process we've shared moments of honesty, amazing dialogue and seen glimpses into one another's hearts. Those moments and conversations have been so meaningful. Thank you. And thank you for Samuel. I didn't know my heart had the capacity to expand the way it did when he was born. I love you three with all of my heart.

To my sisters and brother Diana, Shawn and Amber (and their families — my family): I'm so grateful that we get to do life together. Thank you for helping me keep it real and for allowing me to share pieces of our stories. Memories can sometimes morph over the years and no one but family can help you keep your stories straight. I love the three of you like nobody's business. Thank you.

To my parents — all three of you: I love each of you so much. I am so grateful that though each of our stories are full of hills and valleys, God gave us one another and that we're still on this adventure called life. Thank you for allowing me to share pieces of our stories. God is Good!

Grandmother: That I get to still address you personally in this book is a gift for which I am beyond grateful. Ninety-seven years looks good on you. We are grateful for every second that we get to have you. Thank you for loving Jesus with all of your being, loving your family unconditionally and for living out that love in real ways.

To P.G. & Wilma: You will forever be our friends, confidants and pastors. The Lord brought us together at just the right time. Your unconditional love and care for us have made us feel like mountain-movers! Wilma, thank you for reading pages and cheering me on. (And P.G. — Thank you for letting me share sermon points.) Can't wait for your book!) Thank you.

Ronda: BFC and encourager: I don't remember life before you because we've always been family, but I also don't know how I would have made it without you in recent years as we have walked out our lives and our faith on the same road. You are a connector, a Woman of God and have given me more insight and clarity than you know. Thank you.

Mindy: The way you serve Jesus in everything you do is astounding. You might think you've helped me by diving into this book and getting in the weeds with me — and you did. You might also think you've helped me by giving me a job and a place to use my creative outlet — which would also be true. You might think your friendship has been one of the greatest blessings of my life — and you would be right. While all of these and more are true, what speaks to me most is your life, lived out. You have opened my eyes to what a life lived for Christ truly looks like. Thank you.

June: My sweet friend. Thank you for praying for me and with me, for our visit to the cemetery and all of our conversations about God's faithfulness. Thank you for crying with me as we read through the first chapter I fleshed out. You reassured me that it was time. You exemplify a what it means to be woman of faith. You & Gary are both precious to me — #needprayer?

Kelli & Vince: No one could imagine how much our lives have intersected over these last few years. But God. I am more grateful than words can say to both of you and for more reasons than your being two of my biggest cheerleaders. You have both contributed to this work and into my life. Your friendship is priceless to me. Thank you.

Nancy!!! Nancy Hulshult: Thank you for pushing me! For the questions, for asking me to dive more deeply, for insisting on more detail. It was in my mind, I just needed to get it out. I thank God for you!

Greg Moore: We talked about the concept of this book over appetizers. Your instant interest gave me hope. When I sent my first draft your honesty, which was written across the top of the page, "Stream of consciousness," compelled me to dig deeper. Thank you.

Christina Tedesco: Thank you for meeting me for dinner. Before I began, you encouraged me that my story is one that could help others. That meeting was confirmation to me that it is time. Thank you.

Alli, sister of the heart: You have encouraged, yea even pushed me at times, to get this done. Your joy and exuberance have made me think I could accomplish writing or climbing Kilimanjaro! Thank you for the early readings. Even more, thank you for allowing me to share a part of your story within these pages. You are brave, fearless and courageous. Thank you.

Jules: My prayer partner and friend. Your weekly, sometimes daily query, "The book?" helped me push forward and finish strong! Your friendship and partnership in Jesus is one of the greatest blessings to me. Thank you for always having my back while on your knees in prayer. Thank you.

Dennis: Thank you for being one of the first readers, but more than that, our friend for life. We love you! Thank you.

Amberly Dawn: What a brave Woman of God you are! You have graciously shared parts of your story with me so that together, we can be The Church. Thank you.

Lisa Hawkins: remember? When we first came to ECM you confirmed exactly what I needed to do. Your obedience in hearing Him speak and sharing with me was right on. Your encouragement and love is a blessing to our lives. Thank you.

Eric Ferris: I thought you were gonna be "just a client"! No way! Your partnership in business and ministry has been nothing short of amazing and inspiring. Your early read-through and succinct, excellent advice I have taken to heart and implanted. Thank you.

Bryson & Rachel: I thank God for you! Thank you for the last minute read throughs and encouragement! I love you both!! Thank you.

Lord, You are the Master Weaver. You weave our lives together in a beautiful fabric — a tapestry of Your grace. Thank you. I love you with my life.

UNLIKELY GRACE

THIS IS MY STORY, THIS IS MY SONG: REFLECTIONS, REVELATIONS & HONEST QUESTIONS FOR THE CHURCH I LOVE.

About the Author iii

1. Silverware Revelations 5
2. A Little History 15
3. Normal, Just Like Perfect, Is a Mirage 23
4. Oh, The Blood of Jesus 35
5. About the Birds — Part 1 45
6. A Love of Another Kind — Part 1 49
7. My Tribe 59
8. A Love of Another Kind — Part 2 69
9. Love is a Wonderful Thing 75

Part 2

10. A New Mind 89
11. About the Birds — Part 2 97
12. A Light in the Light 103
13. Shame Off 109
14. God is For Us 121
15. Behind the Veil 129
16. Make Room 137
17. The Danger of Pedestals 145
18. About the Birds — Part 3 157
19. Upon Reflection 167
20. Silverware Reflections 173
21. Food for Thought 177

ABOUT THE AUTHOR

There are millions of people with story's that need to be told and heard. Stories that glorify the greatness of God. Stories that will make a difference in someone's life.

There are also millions of people smarter than me, who have more knowledge of the Bible, who understand types and shadows and scripture much better than me, yet:

...the Spirit teaches you everything you need to know, and what he teaches is true—it is not a lie.
—1 John 2:27b

My heart is for people. My heart is for *The Church*. My hope in sharing my story is that we, *The Church*, will be stirred *and* changed. That we will be moved with compassion toward people — without shame, judgment or regret.

I pray for awakening. I pray that we will move forward *with* Jesus. A wise person recently shared with me this truth: Moving forward seems simple enough, but if we're not following Jesus, we could move forward, right off of a cliff.

Jesus, we Your Church want to follow You.

Disclaimer: all accounts are true, according to my memory. Some of the accounts include information and details from my prayer journals and other's recollections. Any misinformation is unintentional and does not affect the purpose of this account of God's provisions and blessings. Some details in my story have been made intentionally vague to protect very real people.

Chapter 1

SILVERWARE REVELATIONS

In a wealthy home some utensils are made of gold and silver, and some are made of wood and clay. The expensive utensils are used for special occasions, and the cheap ones are for everyday use. If you keep yourself pure, you will be a special utensil for honorable use. Your life will be clean, and you will be ready for the Master to use you for every good work.
—2 Timothy 2:20-21

Reaching into my silverware drawer one morning, the Lord began to speak to my heart about *The Church*. It seems like an odd place to have a spiritual revelation, but quite often He speaks to me using everyday life experience. *Does He speak that way to you?*

Sitting down to process what the Lord was teaching me in that moment, I began to write, contemplating *The Church* and its impact on my life. The more I wrote, the more I wanted to explore this entity, *The Church*, of which I am a part.

I asked myself questions like: *Who are we, The Church?* And even more, *What am I doing as a part of this collective, The Church?* I began to contemplate further as I reflected on my own, personal silverware journey.

SMALL BEGINNINGS

My husband and I purchased silverware — well, flatware — many years ago when it was just the two of us. One set of silverware and a few serving spoons were all we needed for our small household. All the pieces matched and they all fit into one drawer. Perfect. It was the sturdy kind of silverware that has never rusted, tarnished or bent. In fact, even now it looks like it has hardly been used at all.

A few years later, when we started hosting Thanksgiving dinners for our collective families, David's parents purchased us some additional pieces. More of the exact same pattern — enough to open a second location in another drawer! Our silverware stock had grown. It was all the same type, perfectly matching, nesting together quite nicely.

Like most people, once we owned it, I never really gave our silverware a second thought, though we use it every day. The only time I really noticed the silverware was when it was ALL dirty and I had to do dishes just to use a spoon. Over the years we have lost a few pieces here and there to natural attrition... a potluck dinner, a garbage disposal incident, perhaps a serving spoon that made it to the local landfill after the unfortunate Thanksgiving episode of 2005. I jest. We have lost a few pieces, but for the most part, the silverware drawers have stayed intact and relatively unnoticed.

Until recently. My husband's parents health declined in such a way that they needed to move in with us. This has been one of the greatest joys of my life. Don't misunderstand, there are many moments of learning coupled with moments of frustration for us all, but by the grace and the goodness of God, we're doing it. We are becoming a blended family. Along with Grandma and Pawpaw, as I call them, come a myriad of belongings. An untold number of that myriad, I have learned, is silverware.

THE MIGRATION

As we began this process of combining households, Grandma mentioned her silverware to me several times. She wanted to do anything to contribute to the household — to give of what she had. I seem to remember muttering something along the lines of, "We don't need it, we've got plenty."

I was reluctant to bring it into the household at first: 1) because I didn't think we needed it and 2) because it didn't match what was already in the drawer. Heck, their pieces of silverware didn't even match each other. I did not want it!

Shortly after the migration from their house to ours was in full swing, I had to go out of town for a few days. While I was away, the dish washing got behind. Apparently there was a spoon-shortage emergency in the Chaney household! After my husband spent a good twenty minutes looking for a clean utensil, the only logical thing, in his mind, was to bring over the silverware from his parent's house and add it to our collection.

When I got home, my worst fears were confirmed. There it sat, in bags on the counter. Through gritted teeth, I reluctantly put it into the drawers, just to get it out of my way. I didn't want it, didn't need it and I was not excited about it — in any way.

Once I got it all put away, Grandma sweetly reminded that she hadn't had the chance to wash the silverware before it made the trip. I had just mixed unclean silverware into the clean silverware drawer. Which meant that the silverware that I didn't want in the first place, was touching silverware that was already clean.

Emptying the drawers, I cleaned it all — the silverware, the trays and the inside of both drawers. Once sanitized, every piece was ready for circulation. The work was done. I would just learn to live with it.

A few days later I was trying to finish up packing and cleaning at Grandma and Pawpaw's house. Much to my amazement (you guessed it) I found more silverware.

I gave up at that point. I brought what I thought was the rest of the silverware to the commune we were building. This time, I washed it before mobilizing it for service. By now, the trays were spilling over and the drawers were beginning to be hard to open, especially for Grandma and Pawpaw. The weight the new silverware added was remarkable. The drawers — and the silverware — had become a force to be reckoned with.

I was getting used to the new silverware normal when, one more trip to the old house revealed yet another stash of cutlery. (I think Grandma and Pawpaw must have had stock in Oneida or something.) We now have so much silverware that we should never run out, even if I didn't wash dishes for a month.

It *is* a beautiful sight to behold.

I didn't see it that way until the morning of my revelation. I reached into drawer number one for a spoon. For the first time I really looked at all the different pieces of silverware, together. There are pieces that I can't identify. If they have an official name, I don't know it. Some pieces have a beautiful, fancy stem. Some look antique, some brand new. Some are heavy, others feel light and easy to use in my hand... and it truly is a beautiful sight.

Why did I fight bringing the silverware over? Why was I against merging together different pieces from different households? Was it because it would rock my perfectly matching world? We can reason away about the stresses of merging households and all of that, but the truth is, I wanted control of that little corner of my world. I liked it the way it was and had always been and I didn't want change.

As I said earlier, if we are paying attention, The Lord is often revealing Truth to us, and often in the simplest forms. The revelation I had wasn't about merging households or me relinquishing control of my silverware drawer. There are many layers to what He was showing me that day, but the one that resonates the loudest to me is this:

Doesn't my silverware drawer now reflect what *The Church* should look like?

Many of us like "same". We like everything to look the same, feel the same. We like it when all the colors coordinate. Quite often, same makes us comfortable. Yet when I look at the silverware drawer I see this beautiful myriad of different. Not very many pieces look alike anymore. They no longer perfectly nest together yet somehow, they all fit. They've come together to serve this blended household. Though many look and feel different, together they all serve one purpose.

I wonder if we *The Church* can begin to grasp the truth in this silverware revelation?

> *Anyone with ears to hear must listen to the Spirit and understand what he is saying to the churches.*
> *—Revelation 2: 7a, 11a, 17a & 29 | Revelation 3:6, 13 & 22*

WAKE UP CALL

One evening, I was having dinner with a friend. We were catching up on life as it had been some time since we'd seen one another. She was explaining to me that she and her husband had been eating out a lot due to their crazy schedules. While frequenting so many restaurants they seemed to encounter the same people quite often. Then she asked me a question that I will never forget.

"What's up with all the queers around here?"

My breath caught in my chest. I was so taken back that I didn't know what to say. I didn't say anything. I wince every time I remember the conversation. Why didn't I say, "What??? What are you saying? C'mon, let's go to the last place you ate. Let's get to know them. Let's try to reach out. Let's invite them to dinner …" But I didn't. Say. A. Word.

I fear that many times we who have grown up in church are almost conditioned or programmed to "set ourselves apart" and think we are doing the "righteous" thing. I've seen with my own eyes how this friend has shown the love of Christ to many, oftentimes rearranging her own life to minister to someone in need. So what is it that makes us draw the line with certain people?

> *Later, Levi invited Jesus and his disciples to his home as dinner guests, along with many tax collectors and other disreputable sinners. (There were many people of this kind among Jesus' followers.) But when the teachers of religious law who were Pharisees saw him eating with tax collectors and other sinners, they asked his disciples, "Why does he eat with such scum?"*
>
> *When Jesus heard this, he told them, "Healthy people don't need a*

doctor — sick people do. I have come to call not those who think they are righteous, but those who know they are sinners." —Mark 2:15-17

Before you or I go blaming my friend, let's think about this: Do many of us, whether a part of *The Church* or not, actually embrace those who are not like us? Probably not. It is uncomfortable. It is hard. It doesn't "feel" warm and fuzzy. Certain people just don't fit with us. Sometimes our learned thought process tells us that the "dirt" we "see" others carrying could rub off on us.

Is that *The Church* that Jesus called us to be?

QUESTIONS

Many years ago, my husband and I both began feeling that something was wrong with *The Church* in general. Not necessarily the congregation we were serving, but *The Church* as a whole. We started realizing that Jesus probably wouldn't like many of our churches, let alone attend.

We wondered how many churches had members that were actively loving the myriad of different people. I'm not talking color of skin only, although that was also true. I'm talking about people in all stages of growth, all walks of life, the homeless, the friendless, the abused, the trafficked, the drug addict, the outcasts — the myriad of people — that Jesus himself would be hanging out with. People who need to know not only His love, but that Jesus Himself wants to have relationship with them.

Tax collectors and other notorious sinners often came to listen to Jesus teach. This made the Pharisees and teachers of religious law complain that he was associating with such sinful people — even eating with them!
—Luke 15:1-2

Most relationships begin with an introduction. David and I noticed that *The Church* — and this includes he and I, were not making those introductions to anyone who was different.

The more we poured over the Word, we began realizing that Jesus spent more time outside the walls of the church than inside them. When Jesus went to church — to synagogue — He was generally met with opposition. In church!

We came up with many questions, but not many answers.

Are we *The Church* actively seeking those who aren't like us? Are we willing to risk getting close to them? Can we, *The Church* be mindful enough to understand that we will, at times, need to step out of our comfort zone, in order to reach out to people that don't seem "clean"? Can we lay aside our preconceived ideas in order to show God's love?

Could we, *The Church*, be bold enough to show that love through truth-telling? Sometimes it's easy to show affection and consider it "love". Jesus' love spoke truth — confronting sin and loving the sinner. Could we show the love of Jesus by speaking truth without judgment?

Were we making sure that these precious ones, who aren't like us, get to Jesus and **then** find their place in this gigantic blended family, called *The Church*?

Even if we opened the door for different kinds of people to come into the building, were we in touch with reality enough to know how we needed to minister to each of them? Were we listening to Holy Spirit in order to disciple new Christians before we asked them to serve? Would we be gracious when new Christians took steps backwards or had a momentary lapse in judgment?

> *One of the Pharisees asked Jesus to have dinner with him, so Jesus went to his home and sat down to eat. When a certain immoral woman from that city heard he was eating there, she brought a beautiful alabaster jar filled with expensive perfume. Then she knelt behind him at his feet, weeping. Her tears fell on his feet, and she wiped them off with her hair. Then she kept kissing his feet and putting perfume on them.*
> *When the Pharisee who had invited him saw this, he said to himself, "If this man were a prophet, he would know what kind of woman is touching him. She's a sinner!!" —Luke 7:36-39*

The answers to my silverware questions were beginning to make me uncomfortable. I wasn't looking for opportunities outside of the four-walls of my church building. I wasn't actively building relationships with those not like me. I was not making room for anyone. Had I become so comfortable in my "place" in the church that I had forgotten my beginnings?

THE CHURCH CHANGED MY LIFE

Many years ago *The Church* — my church — took me in at a time when I believed that no church would welcome me. My people — my church people — walked me through some of the most confusing, devastating times of my life. Had those people who were being *The Church* not been there, I honestly don't know what my life would look like.

For better or worse, *The Church* has been a part of my life, well, all of my life. I have had an on again/off again, love/hate relationship with what I thought *The Church* should be. That relationship is changing still today. Like any healthy relationship, there are moments of up and downs, but through it all that relationship continues to grow, deepen and be strengthened through Jesus.

This is not a book about me, yet it is. I can only speak from experience — from the places I alone have passed through. My life's journey has been filled with pain and triumph, but I can tell you this: that it is only the grace of God that has kept me. His Mercy has walked me through some dark passageways only to discover another facet of who He is; His Goodness has kept me through my inconsistent choices in order to protect my future; and He has used *The Church* to help me navigate many of those journeys.

My personal story reveals how members of *The Church* didn't turn me away. They held the door open for me to come back in and then they ministered to me. It wasn't a formulated plan. They didn't meet together to decide what to do with me. They each did what Jesus called them to do, what Holy Spirit spoke into their heart. They walked with me as I became whole, ready to serve alongside them, for the glory of God.

God's plan has always been to use His Bride, *The Church*, as a place of grace and truth. Many Jesus followers who attend church want our churches to look like my blended silverware drawer, but we're not sure how to get there. It can be overwhelming to even know where to begin.

This is my heart. To show how a group of believers each did what they were called to do in a single moment or a season of their life. Their love, tenacity and willingness to serve changed my life, forever.

I've never really wanted to share my story. In fact, I've told the Lord a thousand times, *There are many more powerful stories out there. Why tell mine?* He has assured me that my obedience is what matters.

MORE

Are those of us who are a part of *The Church* making room for more? By more I mean, more Jesus followers who might look, smell, act and minister differently from our same?

There are more. More to be found. More to be brought into the household. More to be washed. More to cleaned. More to be put into service. More to make a difference in this world.

It's not about perfection. It's not about staying neat and tidy and fitting into a mold — or a proverbial silverware tray. Jesus never fit the mold. He was wild and His ways were untamed. He was filled with power and demonstrated that power with love. He attracted the different ones, the outcasts, the sinners… and He loved them — loves us — all.

His love made all of the difference for all of time.

> *Jesus traveled through all the towns and villages of that area, teaching in the synagogues and announcing the Good News about the Kingdom. And he healed every kind of disease and illness. When he saw the crowds, he had compassion on them because they were confused and helpless, like sheep without a shepherd. He said to his disciples, "The harvest is great, but the workers are few. So pray to the Lord who is in charge of the harvest; ask him to send more workers into his fields."*
> *—Matthew 9:35*

Are we ready to give more time? Be more present in each moment? Actively look for more opportunities to reach the harvest?

I believe we *The Church* are beginning to sense the urgency to move beyond the walls of our buildings to be the hands, feet and heart of Jesus to our broken communities —all around the world.

Are we ready to follow Jesus' example? Through Him, a church was born that, "the gates of hell will never conquer".

My prayer is that we, *The Church*, will awaken. That we will take up His cause. That we will realize that we ARE the laborers He has chosen to use in this harvest. Being a part of *The Church* in this way probably won't look like what we're used to, but we get to be in on what The Lord is doing.

Through this awakening, I pray that more people can meet Jesus. More lives can be given the hope, relationship and love they seek. More Jesus followers will become an active part of this mighty, moving force we call *The Church*.

MUSIC NOTES: Music is and has been such a huge part of my life. The Lord uses music to speak to me, minister to me, refresh me and make me think. I wanted to place song lyrics within the body of my story, but I never want to infringe on the rights of others. The easiest and best way to share with you both the lyrics and possibly the experience, is to share song titles and the links to find these songs on YouTube or in iTunes. I hope that you'll take a minute to listen if you haven't heard these songs and I hope that you will honor each writer, publisher and performer by purchasing the songs if you want to put them in your playlist.

MUSIC NOTES, CH 1: If there were ever a song that I felt depicted my life, it would probably be *If Not For Your Grace*, as recorded by Israel Houghton and New Breed. From the moment I heard it I wondered if Aaron & Israel knew my story, but as Christians, we are each recipients of that restoring, redeeming, amazing grace.

Find it on YouTube at: https://youtu.be/pahwV5mwK40 or in iTunes at: https://music.apple.com/us/album/a-deeper-level/641413484

Songwriters: Aaron Lindsey / Israel Houghton
If Not For Your Grace lyrics © Warner Chappell Music, Inc, Capitol Christian Music Group

Chapter 2

A LITTLE HISTORY

A LITTLE LAUGHTER FOR THOSE OF US WHO GREW UP IN CHURCH & SOME CONTEXT FOR THOSE WHO DIDN'T

In and out of church until I was in my 20's when I finally stayed, I've had a lot of church experience. When I was young, I didn't see *The Church* for the richness it had to offer. All I knew is this: I was definitely supposed to be there and I didn't want to go to hell. The church I most remember was small yet vibrant, located on the outskirts of my hometown.

My grandparents took my sister and me to church most of our childhood. My parents didn't go to church with us for quite a while. I now know that some of the rules and regulations of church in those days played a role in their avoidance.

For instance, when my mom was a teenager she was exuberant about being involved at church. She recalls volunteering for an activity and being frowned upon because she wore pants. She was humiliated and didn't want to return. Wearing pants, using makeup or having earrings shouldn't have been an issue, but in that day, it was for many. It took almost 10 years for her to go back to church after that incident.

My dad, on the other hand, grew up in church but had an abusive father who was an active member in that church. Dad and his siblings lived with the "you should know better than that" shame from him, among many other things. I don't blame my dad for not wanting to live in that abuse, let alone go to church and pretend that everything was okay.

My parents got married at a very young age. Though they both had church in their backgrounds, it wasn't a part of their lives in the early years of their marriage, but they didn't mind if my sister and I went.

For me, church was a safe place. Between the ages of five and eleven, I "got saved"[1] probably 15 or 20 times. There were a couple of reasons for this. Looking back, I think I was a rotten kid and I kind of knew it. Let me clarify my reasoning.

SPEAKING OF ROTTEN — REASON NUMBER ONE

Being the oldest, I lorded over my little sister constantly. Anyone who knows me now knows that I cherish my sister and we are very close, but for some reason when we were growing up, I viewed her as younger and unknowledgeable in every way. She was so sweet and naive that it was easy for me to take advantage of her — and I did.

Diana had fingernails sharper than cat claws and there were several instances where my arms experienced the puncture wounds that only a she-fight could bring. Generally the wounds were in retaliation for my tormenting her, like punching *at* her face but stopping just before impact. Terrified, she would brace for pain, but I never actually hit her — at least not during those moments of torture.

One summer my sister got to go to church youth camp without me. I couldn't go because I had cut my heel playing ditch (see circa 1970s outdoor games). While she was away at camp I stole her gum balls. All of them. She had a little gum ball machine — where the user was supposed to put in coins and get back a gum ball. I loved gum balls. Couple that with the fact that I had zero respect for my little sister and it didn't look good for her gum ball machine. I hacked into it — no money — and chewed all of her gumballs while she was away at camp, without any intention of ever paying her back.[2]

I was so sneaky. I snuck when I had no reason to sneak. I snuck to do almost anything I wanted. I stole. I stole lunch money from other kids' desks in the 2nd grade and then of course, lied about it.

As we got a little older, our parents both worked full-time jobs and had other things going on so quite often Diana and I were alone. Back then the neighbors all knew each other and family was always close, so being alone wasn't a big deal... except that I figured out ways to get what I wanted when no one was around.

In the 5th grade, a friend and I would gang up on a fellow classmate and punch her — just because we could. Then there was the 5th grade cussing streak. I remember discovering bad words and saying them all the time at school. I guess that went along with being tough and beating up helpless classmates. My life was on a trajectory of rottenness, even in the 5th grade. Because I went to church, my limited understanding of grace meant that my being rotten wasn't getting me a pass into heaven.

My dad didn't have a boy child at that point — my little brother didn't come along for another 6 or 7 years, so I became Daddy's "boy" in a way and I loved every moment. I adored my dad and spending time with him was my favorite thing.

We shared the love of music. We were singing all the time. He was learning to play the guitar. Music and singing was a huge part of our lives — and if dad was learning to play, so would I.

He taught me to competitively play football, softball and basketball. It wasn't just playing. Dad taught me everything he knew about each of the sports. He signed me up to participate in any sport a girl could play in the '70s, like softball and basketball. No real football for girls, so I played touch football with the neighborhood kids. It was a blast! I was usually the only girl, but I was pretty good so I got respect.

One time in the 5th grade, I had a huge crush on my neighbor, Mike. I wanted him to like me, so I tried to do some things he and other friends suggested. I stopped wearing toboggans all the time and tried to brush my hair and well, look like a girl. All of that fuss ended up not being worth it to me. My hair was a mess. It was like a hair pyramid. I didn't know how to do all of that girly stuff either so I let it go and embraced my tomboy ways, which led to another seed being planted in me a few years later.

I also remember thinking impure thoughts — even that young. I was exposed to some things that a child shouldn't know. Things my parents don't even know about. As young as 7-and 8-years old, though I didn't understand and couldn't process what was happening, I knew that some of the thoughts I had were sensual. In my mind all of that was dirty, so I was dirty.

Still on reason number one here, I got "saved" all the time was because I knew I was a rotten kid who did rotten things. I knew enough about God to know that there was no way a loving God was ever going to let me go to heaven because I messed up. I did wrong every day. Heaven was a place I for sure wanted to go. I did not want to get left behind.

I'LL DO IT!! REASON NUMBER TWO

The second reason for all my "savings" I now realize was a preview into the codependent tendencies I was developing. Looking back, I can see that my natural instinct to assume responsibility for everyone's happiness and success began at an early age.

At church after almost every sermon, the Pastor or visiting minister would call for people to come forward and pray. If no one came forward for salvation, especially for the visiting minister, I felt it was my responsibility to fulfill their mission. Top that with my view of myself — a rotten kid who did rotten things — what did I have to lose? In my young mind, it couldn't hurt to get saved — again. I didn't recognize the beginnings of misplaced guilt. I still had much to learn and had no concept of a grace that lasts. In my limited understanding, God's grace had a very short shelf-life when applied to me.

SO MANY MEMORIES

Still, I have so many memories of that little church. I'm so grateful to Grandmother for getting us there. One vivid memory I have is kneeling down to pray at the altar and my yellow dress surrounding me — almost as if it were a dream. The significance of that moment sticks in my mind as one where I really prayed and experienced the presence of the Lord. I remember Bible drills where we would learn to find the verses the fastest. I was so competitive and I loved Bible drills so much, yet I didn't realize that those drills were laying the foundation of my knowledge of scripture. I remember Sunday school lessons, flannelgraphs[5] and songs about Zaccheus and Abraham.

In fact, the "big church"[6] song service was one of my favorite moments every week. We sang out of the red back hymnal.[7] I loved it so much that I knew the page numbers by heart. Page 92: *Just a Little Talk with Jesus*; Page 10: *Meeting in the Air*; Page 33: *I'll Fly Away* and so many more became part of the foundation of my beliefs. Music, singing and worship were woven into my being in that little church.

Often we would have Testimony Night. Anyone and everyone in church was given the opportunity to stand up and tell what the Lord had done for them that week. With pure sincerity many testimonies sounded like this: "Pray for me. The devil's after me, it's been a hard week but God is good..." Perhaps this practice came from our Appalachian tradition, but I loved getting to hear real people tell the stories of how God met their need or ministered to them. Many of us who have grown up in or around church can hear it now! What a faith-building practice!

> **SIDE STORY**
> One afternoon, after recently seeing, A *Thief in the Night*,[3] at church, my sister and I came home from school to an empty house. We called Grandmother — no answer. We called Sister Johnson (our pastor's wife) — no answer. We looked in the phone book and found other church members to call — no answer. Diana and I began to panic, knowing that the Rapture had taken place and we had been left behind![4] We couldn't believe it — we knew we were saved!! (Me probably for the 3rd or 15th time by then.) I think we finally got a hold of Grandmother and all was right with the world. We were relieved and we rejoiced — for the moment.

I was about nine-or ten-years old when I knew I was ready to share on Testimony Night. That particular Sunday, the morning service had included baby dedications. My sister, Diana, had not been dedicated as infant so she was one of the children who were dedicated that morning. I'm sure it was a little awkward for her, being an eight-year-old among mostly babies.

Sunday night came. I stood up, heart pounding planning to confess my love for the Lord in front of the whole church — and I did! However, I don't remember one word I said, because my little sister stood up next and upstaged me with five simple words: "I felt funny being dedicated." The whole church roared. I don't think I spoke aloud in church again for years.

THE LOVE OF A GRANDMOTHER

I actually adore(d) both of my grandmas. I was and am so very blessed to have had both of them pour into my life.

My mom's mom, Anna Baker, was a piece of every part of my life until she passed away 30 years ago. I was her first grandchild and her love for me was fierce. She and Grandpa Baker treated me like their own child and provided for me time and time again. She taught me how to speak truth, love well and embrace life to the fullest. I miss her dearly.

My grandma Ayers, Helen, who I call Grandmother, is the one who made sure we were at church as much as she could during those formative years. As far as I can remember she gave me my first Bible. A little white, leather-bound King James Version that I carried constantly for many years. I studied that Bible, wrote in it and used it regularly. I won't go as far as to say daily because as an 11-or 12-year old, I really don't remember reading daily. I just remember loving it so much. I cherished that Bible, carried it to church and longed to learn its truth. I memorized a lot of scripture in that little KJV. And when I got older, I gave it away. But that's another story.

Each Sunday and sometimes on Wednesdays, either my grandparents or the church bus picked us up and took us to church. In the early years, I remember Grandmother taking First National Bank notepads and pens so we could have something to do during the sermon. Certs® and half-pieces of Wrigley's Gum were a treat if we behaved.

When we were at church, the Word was being planted in our hearts, though we were actively writing

ANOTHER STORY
After David and I married, we moved to Tennessee while he finished school. Through my job I met a young woman who was also young in her faith. She had so many questions and no access to a Bible. Feeling prompted by Holy Spirit, I gave her my little white Bible, notes and all. It's been many years now, but I know that the word of Lord, "always produces fruit.... it will prosper everywhere (He) sends it," (Isaiah 55:11). I pray she and her family are thriving.

notes, drawing pictures or chewing gum. We were there. Grandmother got us to the one place she knew would eventually make a difference. Even in that small town church, where legalism seemed to rule the day, I was able to learn about Jesus. As a rule, most were sincere in teaching others what they knew about Jesus. I especially remember fondly the women in the church. They were giving their very the best. He did the rest.

> *Let the message about Christ, in all its richness, fill your lives. Teach and counsel each other with all the wisdom he gives. Sing psalms and hymns and spiritual songs to God with thankful hearts. And whatever you do or say, do it as a representative of the Lord Jesus, giving thanks through him to God the Father. —Colossians 3:16-17*

Church wasn't the only place Grandmother made sure we were cared for. After my parent's divorce, my dad, my sister and I moved in with Grandmother and Grandpa. Had they not allowed us to do so, I'm not sure how we would have made it. They helped us more than I ever knew.

Grandmother was and is a pivotal part of my life to this day.

Grandmother taught me how to pray — right there at the living room couch while Grandpa had the news blaring in the TV room. She taught me not only how to pray, but how to listen to the Lord and how to read and study the Word.

Grandmother taught me how to worship. On that same living room couch, sometimes with the guitar, sometimes not, we would sing out of that red back hymnal, adding a few worship choruses here and there — there were not many back then — but she taught me that we only had an audience of One, and He deserves all of our worship, no matter the style or kind of music.

Grandmother taught Diana and me how to cook, how to keep peace, how to love others and how to share Jesus with them by living a godly life.

Grandmother, who is at this writing, 97-years-old, gives the Lord glory for everything in her life and she taught us to do the same. I would love to say that I was the only one she did all of that for, but that wouldn't be true. Many of my cousins, the ones from my generation especially, had the same experiences that I did with a Grandmother who laid the groundwork for her grandchildren to become *The Church*.

I don't remember many kids, if any, being brought to church by their grandparents back then, but I was. Though that little church where I began seemed to have many rules — no pants, no earrings, no makeup for women — there were people in it, including my

Grandmother, who understood that knowing Jesus was more than a set of "dos & don'ts".

My sister and I would show up at church reeking of cigarette smoke and desperation, which, if we're being honest, is often a repellent. It's hard to get involved in a messed up kid's life. Yet, there were men and women in *The Church* who showed us more grace and more truth than we could understand.

I am forever grateful for Grandmother and for the people that somehow got beyond the rules of religious traditions. They truly knew a Savior and they wanted Diana and me to know Him too. Somehow they made room for us. They got beyond a legalistic way of thinking and made sure that these two children knew there was more joy to this faith-walk than we could ever imagine. They were and are *The Church*.

[1]*Getting Saved: means going forward to the altar to pray and accept Jesus as my Savior.*

[2]*At a recent speaking engagement, I repaid Diana publicly for the gumballs — machine and all.*

[3]*A Thief in the Night is a 1972 evangelical Christian film written by Jim Grant directed and produced by Donald W. Thompson, and starring Patty Dunning as Patty Myers, the main character and protagonist, along with Thom Rachford, Colleen Niday and Mike Niday in supporting roles. It is the first installment in the Thief in the Night series about the Rapture, Tribulation, and Second Coming of Christ. The film is set during the near future, focusing on Patty, a young woman who was not raptured and who struggles to decide what to do in the face of the Tribulation.*

[4]*Songwriter: Larry Norman ©1969*
I Wish We'd All Been Ready lyrics © Sony/ATV Music Publishing LLC

[5]*Flannelgraph: Is a board covered with flannel fabric used in Sunday School for illustrating a story. The characters and scenery consisted of paper, which easily stuck the flannel, but could be moved around as the lesson is taught.*

[6]*Big Church: Is referring to the church service held in the main sanctuary. Generally the adults have church in the main sanctuary while the children have Children's Church where the service is geared specifically for them.*

[6]*The Red Back Hymnal is actually called Church Hymnal and was created by Pathway Press. It called "Red Back" because of the cloth color. Church members had access to them at almost every seat or sometimes they could share. They used the book during the congregational singing, allowing them to be able to sing along. Visit https://redbackhymnal.com/ for a fun look at this historic book.*

MUSIC NOTES, CH 2: *I Wish We'd All Been Ready* was the theme song from the movie *A Thief in the Night*. Larry Norman was one of the pioneers of Christian rock and Jesus music.

Find it on YouTube at: https://youtu.be/Ep4Aj-kJkJM or in iTunes by DCTalk (an amazing cover) at: https://music.apple.com/us/album/i-wish-wed-all-been-ready/723622363?i=723623228

Chapter 3

NORMAL – JUST LIKE PERFECT – IS A MIRAGE
AND OTHER FUN MYTHS

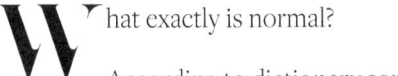

What exactly is normal?

According to dictionary.com:[1]

nor•mal
adjective
1. conforming to a standard; usual, typical, or expected.
"it's quite normal for puppies to bolt their food"

noun
1. the usual, average, or typical state or condition.
"her temperature was above normal"

Words — and the study of words fascinates me. Perspectives and various word usages tend to morph or even become distorted over time, so I like to look at their history and usages. I looked up the definition of normal on the Urban Dictionary website.[2] Say what you want about it, but there is a generation that identifies with the definitions found there.

According to the Urban Dictionary, normal is:

o   A word made up by this corrupt society so they could single out and attack those who are different.
o   The meaning is constantly evolved to suit the momentary desires and/or needs of a single person, or group of people.
o   There is no such thing as normal so there really can't be a definition......

Let that sink in. *No such things as normal....*

I grew up, like so many others, thinking that my family was the odd family and that all other families were normal. I smile as I write those words. The ever elusive normal is a deep longing for many.

SEEKING PERFECTION

There was also a time that I felt everything in my life had to be perfect or else it was wrong. Along with our pursuit of "normal" many of us also have the compulsion for perfection.

Whatever drives those of us who desire perfection is as individual and unique as we are. Regret? Self Importance? Insecurity? Anxiety? Fear? Fear of loss, fear of failure, fear of rejection, fear of not being enough, fear of not having love or being loved, fear of being wrong, fear of {insert your own adverb here}.

By striving for perfection in our homes, in our families, in our looks or in our relationships are we really living honestly? Are we really being true to who God has purposed us to be?

I was pondering perfection one morning, even as I was finishing this book. That word means so many things to different people. The Lord brought to my mind these words "the yoke of perfection". The picture became clear.[3]

A yoke is a wooden beam or crosspiece that is fitted over two animals, such as oxen, then attached to a plow or cart. The yoke was meant to distribute the weight evenly, so that neither animal was bearing the entire load.

Over time, the word yoke has evolved to mean "an oppressive agency" or being kept down by the weight of injustice.[4]

The yoke of perfection is real. As if many of us didn't carry it before, in the last 15 years our ability to see into the lives of others has made this yoke exponentially tighter and heavier. Picture perfect homes, lives and faces are portrayed for the world to see, while what is taking place behind the scenes, hidden from our view is anything but perfect. We buy into an illusion, as we watch, scroll or tap from our less than perfect seat, believing that we indeed are less than.

Jesus said, "...My yoke is easy to bear, and the burden I give you is light." His yoke is not oppressive. And I'm pretty sure if we allow Him, He will bear the weight of our load. Oh that we would always remember these precious words.

But we do forget and often when we fall short, we begin believing the illusion again —

NORMAL, JUST LIKE PERFECT, IS A MIRAGE

everyone else is perfect and I am a complete failure. If we're not careful, then comes the blame: our parents failed us, our families let us down, our schools or church left us lacking... the list can go on and on.

What if we all just stepped back and took another look? Instead of seeing our "lack" of perfection, what if we understood that we don't have to be perfect? What if we allowed one another this grace: It's OK that we are imperfect people from dysfunctional families. All of us.

IS DYSFUNCTION NORMAL?

In spite of my own family's "normal dysfunction" we had some good moments and fond memories. When we were little Diana and I loved to put on shows for our Grandma and Grandpa Baker. Our Aunt Becky, who was only a few years older than us, would help us rehearse and then get into costume. Diana was the dancer, I was the singer. Perfoming at the living room fireplace, our stage name was "The Nutty Buddies". We were lip-sync professionals way before Milli or Vanilli!

We also had wonderful celebrations with extended family on Grandma Ayers' side. Gigantic family reunions where many of her 12 sibling's families and their families would gather. My aunts and uncles, even some of my cousins would play music and we would sing and feast... so many good memories.

My cousin, Kenny and I were very close, though he lived what seemed like a million miles away and we only got to spend time together at family reunions and on rare visits. I think he took me under his wing because he and his family could see the turmoil Diana and I were living in.

Blended families are hard. Period. Couple that with the internal issues that both my dad and stepmom fought as individuals, blending that altogether became a hot mess. The verbal abuse that Diana and I took was often unleashed in front of others. Many could see it and felt helpless to intervene — but not my Aunt Phyllis, who was Kenny's mom.

Aunt Phyl was a force to be reckoned with. She gave me lots of fun advice and offered that I could come live with them in Alabama. I was so tempted to move. Throughout my life I've often wished I would have, but I couldn't leave dad. It meant so much to me that someone tried to help me, even validating that I, in all my teenageriness, wasn't totally to blame for the household turmoil which I thought was my fault. In hindsight, perhaps it would have been for the best, but I had Daddy issues. Let me explain.

#abandonmentissues

Going back a few years, I was 11 when my parents divorced. In our situation, it was my mom who left. I was Daddy's girl anyway and would have fought to stay with him no matter what, but Mom felt it was time for a new start. Was I angry, absolutely. Am I now? No. The grace of God of allows us to see life through a clean lens.

Through the divorce, dad and I grew even closer. Of course I didn't realize it at the time, but I think I became his surrogate best friend. He talked to me about all of his goings on and I just listened. That's what I was supposed to do, right? He talked me about dates he went on, perhaps trying to see if we liked any of the women he dated. He shared some of his struggles in that season of life, including financial pressures. At the age of 12 that heavy load was my normal, but I was OK. I could handle it. That's when I began to take on the role of rescuer.

Dad loved us and cared for us the best he knew how. We moved out of Grandmother's house into our own apartment. Just the three of us. And dad was there for us. He held us when Diana and I would cry in the night, not being able to articulate the gaping wound of abandonment we felt. He did fun things with us that didn't cost a dime. We listened to music on our 8-track player and danced and sang. He took us to a new church that had a vibrant youth ministry, making sure we were there every week. Those trips to church are where my relationship with Jesus really began to grow.

When I was twelve, I had a spiritual experience at church that I will never forget. I was at the altar praying when I began to pray in the Spirit. I spoke in tongues and cried an almost grieving cry. My dad carried me out of the church, laid me in the

SIDE STORY

Not long after I got married I went to counseling. There were just some issues I needed to deal with and thankfully the church where my husband worked had a full-time counselor. We began diving into my past and one of the first things he addressed were Daddy issues that I didn't even realize I had! My counselor told me to write a letter to my dad, telling him the ways I felt abandoned and hurt, so I did. I really poured my heart out in honesty.

I went back to counseling the following week and the counselor asked to read my letter.

"What letter?" I asked.

"The one you wrote to your dad," he replied.

I gulped. My stomach dropped to my knees.

"I mailed it," I said flatly. My counselor almost fainted. I think I missed the part where he instructed me to, "Bring it back next week." Oops.

But the letter actually opened a door of healing between dad and me. The Lord has really blessed our relationship and Little Mommy, my dad's wife of almost 30 years now, has been a great encourager in our healing. She's always encouraging me to "take my part." And so I try.

backseat of the car and drove me home. I later understood that this whole experience was healing for me. Romans 8:26 in action:

> *And the Holy Spirit helps us in our weakness. For example, we don't know what God wants us to pray for. But the Holy Spirit prays for us with groanings that cannot be expressed in words. —Romans 8:26*

Dad was not perfect, but I didn't know that. He was my hero. Not many men in that day took their children to raise, especially daughters, but he did. I adored him for that. It was the three of us and we didn't know that anything was not "normal".

Once he began dating his soon-to-be second wife however, everything changed. We changed churches and began attending her church. After they were married, in the span of one year I moved three times. Suddenly all of dad's attention and affection went to his new wife at her demand. I remember one morning at breakfast, shortly after the wedding, she made this announcement:

"Now that your dad and I are married, He loves me first. You are now second to him. The Bible says that's the way it is supposed to be, so that's the way it will be from now on."

In a marriage that is the way it should be, right? Putting your spouse first? Yet that's where the tricky blended family thing comes in. In her insecurities and her quest for real love, my stepmother confused this truth with levels of love, instead of this biblical precedence to show your children how to love. In hindsight, I see that she felt threatened, especially where I was concerned. Who was I to argue with God's Word? If He said husbands are supposed to love their wives first, what could I say? He's God!

I thought she hated me and maybe she did, but again, in hindsight, I recognize there were a lot of fragments in her thinking that stemmed from brokenness in her own life that hadn't been addressed, let alone healed. I later learned that my stepmom's "normal" had included being in an abusive relationship earlier in her life.

In the early years of their marriage, I tried to be close with her, but every attempt was met with pain. We really needed family therapy. I tried out calling her "Mom" once, just trying it on to see how it felt. She abrasively told me from that moment on that is what I had to call her, because she couldn't take the back and forth. Now, I understand it, but then, it felt like a punishment.

Dad started working a lot, staying gone, avoiding confrontation — and me — or at least it seemed.

Once again I had abandonment issues. At the age of 13 I began searching for some person to fill that void. I had a relationship with the Lord. He was with me and I knew it. I had wonderful, beautiful experiences in prayer and in church, yet I longed for a human to fill that emotional void.

My worldview became dysfunctional.

DIFFERENT YET THE SAME

Being a Daddy's girl, I was a competitive tomboy who loved sports. For some reason I was more comfortable hanging out with the guys than with most girls.

One crazy hobby we had as kids in our small college town was collecting beer cans. It was all the rage and in my neighborhood the more variety, the better. We did this for fun. We had beer can pyramids in our bedrooms. I remember the really tall ones were especially hard to find. Whoever had the most diverse collection was the winner of the day.

Contrast this to one of my most treasured friendships later in my life. She collected cans too, but she collected them for survival. The more she found, the more she could cash in. The more she could cash in meant that she could eat. My friend lived in the streets, alone at the age of 12.

She had been physically and sexually abused by a family member, only to be turned away by her own mother. To think that my dysfunctional family compares to hers is absurd to me. Yet, neither of us knew any differently.

She was living in the streets while I was in a home, both of us longing for "normal".

At 16 she did what she could to exist, being raped for survival, while I, at 16, began having sex for connection.

The two don't compare. I'm sure she would have traded anything to live my "normal". Yet we were both living in dysfunction created by another's dysfunction, created by another's dysfunction, by another's dysfunction... you get the picture.

Even though we were worlds apart, God knew exactly where each of was. Did He design that we live those lives? No. Yet He was with us. He never left us. Did we each go through hard things? Yes, but we each cried out to Him. He placed people in our paths to help us find our way. People who reached out to us from their "normal" to help us find Him.

We would often say to each other, "How did we make it? How are we leading somewhat "normal" lives?" The truth is we're really not normal at all, but we're no longer trapped in the weight of someone else's choices.

NORMAL, JUST LIKE PERFECT, IS A MIRAGE

The point I'm trying to make is this: do we *The Church* fall for the illusion that life should be normal? Remember the definition of normal: "standard; usual, typical, or expected."

When something doesn't appear "normal" or "perfect" to us, do we look the other way?

When we are filled with compassion towards a person or situation that seems out of the ordinary, do we ignore or push down those feelings? When Jesus asks us to go out of our way to accomplish something for Him, do we say to ourselves, *Oh, that's just me. That's just in my own head. He would never ask me to do anything uncomfortable...*

Friend, I've heard that voice too.

> *Eventually he came to the Samaritan village of Sychar, near the field that Jacob gave to his son Joseph. Jacob's well was there; and Jesus, tired from the long walk, sat wearily beside the well about noontime. Soon a Samaritan woman came to draw water, and Jesus said to her, "Please give me a drink." He was alone at the time because his disciples had gone into the village to buy some food.* —John 4:5-8

Jesus made this stop in Samaria on his way to Galilee. Most Jews avoided Samaria altogether, taking a bypass, making a long journey longer. The prejudice went back centuries. Samaritans were once brothers and sisters to all Jews, descending from the northern kingdom of Israel. For more history on this relationship see 2 Kings 17, Ezra 9 and Nehemiah 13.[5]

For many familiar and unjust reasons, Jews and Samaritans hated one another and would normally go to great lengths to avoid interaction. Period. Scripturally, there is much more here so please, study it for yourself. These passages are just one tiny glimpse into how Jesus worked beyond normal every day.

The bottom line is this: Jesus lovingly crossed racial, gender and religious lines—not "normal".

> *The woman was surprised, for Jews refuse to have anything to do with Samaritans. She said to Jesus, "You are a Jew, and I am a Samaritan woman. Why are you asking me for a drink?"*
>
> *Jesus replied, "If you only knew the gift God has for you and who you are speaking to, you would ask me, and I would give you living water."*
> —John 4:9-10

This woman's "normal" was so fraught with dysfunction, it took her a minute to recognize what Jesus was telling her — the Answer to all of her own thirsts was right in front of her eyes. Could it be that we too are so comfortable in our dysfunction that we happily or unhappily stay there?

What about the disciples vision of normal?

> Just then his disciples came back. They were shocked to find him talking to a woman, but none of them had the nerve to ask, "What do you want with her?" or "Why are you talking to her?"
> —John 4:27

It wasn't only the Pharisees, Sadducees or the religious who didn't understand Jesus or His ways. The people closest to Him couldn't see past their normal either. At this point they didn't know Him or His heart well enough to understand that He didn't care about the social norms of that day.

ANYTHING BUT "NORMAL"

Jesus was anything but normal, so why do we chase after it?

Normal is comfortable and expected. Normal doesn't push us out of our seat to let someone else sit there. Normal doesn't push us to invite someone to lunch, church, conversation, coffee — in order to share the love of Jesus and possibly face rejection.

Normal doesn't force us to speak up about our faith.

Normal doesn't break our hearts to stand up for those who have no voice.

SIDE STORY

Erica and her family were looking for a church. Having left the church they had attended their entire life, they were looking for a good, solid Bible-believing place where they all could plug in, serve and belong.

She and her husband found their new church home in a progressive, lively, active-in-the-community church. It seemed to be forward thinking and accepting of people who look liked them — tattoos, piercings and all.

After attending for a while, Erica decided to dive in and volunteered to serve on the Greeting Team.

She was promptly told to find another area to serve. Erica didn't have "the look" that church leadership wanted greeting people coming through the door.

She and her family of five moved from there. It has been several years and though Erica loves God with all of her heart, they haven't yet found another church home.

Erica says, "I want people to realize ...while some think people who look like me are 'of the devil' in reality we are the nicest people you will ever meet (like nicer than church peeps). We are not perfect (none of us are) but many of us are hurting and tired and just want true friendship and love."

I love you Girl.

Normal doesn't allow us to cross racial, economic or cultural barriers. To embrace different. To not only love like He loves, but also enrich our lives with "different".[6]

Normal looks through one lens. That lens is narrow — too narrow to allow God's possibilities to take us on the adventure He has planned for us.

What about sin? Do we rank sins as "normal" or "average" (according the definition at the beginning of the chapter)? I have done that — but I was wrong. Sin is sin and it all separates us from God. We tend to rank sin by what *we can see*. Even then, most of us don't rank gluttony up there with fornication... but they are both sin and sin separates.

What if we owned up to our imperfections? What if we did as James 5:16 implores us to do?

> *Confess your sins to each other and pray for each other so that you may be healed. The earnest prayer of a righteous person has great power and produces wonderful results. —James 5:16*

What if we humbled ourselves, realizing that this grace-walk needs to renewed regularly? What if we realized that there is no one who is perfect, but He can use us anyway?

> *God alone, who gave the law, is the Judge. He alone has the power to save or to destroy.* **So what right do you have to judge your neighbor?**
> *—James 4:12*

You'll find throughout this book I ask a lot of questions. These are questions I ask myself. I am not perfect — I take ownership of that fact.

Jesus crossed boundaries to get to people. Have you ever allowed something to be a boundary that didn't need to be?

Do we look at people whose outward appearance different from ours and think they are untouchable? We cannot see their heart. Could we possibly even learn a thing or two from those who don't look like us?

What if we put an end to the whispers or gossip we have listened to about "so and so"? Instead, wrapping Jesus' arms — through our own arms — around them?

What if we only saw each other as people — created in the image of God? Each one "fearfully and wonderfully made" in their God-given uniqueness.

What if we didn't shun a person who is gay?

What if we couldn't see the years of trauma someone has suffered that causes them to act out of the ordinary?

What if we see a person who chooses a religion we know nothing about? What will be our response?

Does Jesus love them? Do we? What if we choose not to judge, but rather to love?

Don't put the book down. I'm not saying we shouldn't lovingly confront sin, but there's a time for doing that, and it is as the Lord leads. There's a time to help those we are doing life with deal with issues that are causing them to be separated or to walk away from God. What I am saying is when we judge people by what we see or from the position of a "high-horse", we begin to go down a slippery slope.

Jesus said: "Refuse to be a critic full of bias toward others, and judgment will not be passed on you. For you'll be judged by the same standard that you've used to judge others. The measurement you use on them will be used on you. Why would you focus on the flaw in someone else's life and yet fail to notice the glaring flaws of your own? How could you say to your friend, 'Let me show you where you're wrong,' when you're guilty of even more? You're being hypercritical and a hypocrite! First acknowledge your own 'blind spots' and deal with them, and then you'll be capable of dealing with the 'blind spot' of your friend," Matthew 7:1-5, TPT.

GOD MOMENTS

I'll never forget a God-moment I had one afternoon when the "goth" look was really becoming en vogue. My husband and I went to see a movie with some friends. Across the lobby, I saw a couple of teenagers dressed in dark clothing, dark make up, black nails and all. They were off to themselves as if to say, "Don't come near." I was all too happy to oblige.

Not wanting to get near them, I looked at them as if they had leprosy. My fear of what I didn't know, couldn't understand or see past caused me to judge them without ever hearing them speak one word.

And then I heard a still, small voice. "But I love them."

Still today a lump rises in my throat as I remember that precious moment. I, who had been forgiven of much, dared to look down from my new "normal" on a boy and a girl that Jesus loves. And what's worse, I didn't go to them and tell them that He loves them.

Not a proud moment for me, yet one that began to change my life, my mind and the way

I see, forever.

He loves them.

> *Stop judging based on the superficial. First you must embrace the standards of mercy and truth. —John 7:24 TPT*

Them is me. Them is you.

THE WAY WE SEE

A mirage by definition is an optical illusion: an image, produced by very hot air, of something that seems to be far away but does not really exist.

A second definition, according to the Cambridge Dictionary[7] online is this: a hope or wish that has no chance of being achieved.

A hope or wish that has no chance of being achieved — like "normal" or "perfect".

With Jesus, our dysfunction can become the adventure of a lifetime. I've learned and am learning still to embrace those opportunities and be a part of His adventures.

My formative years were full of odd relationships. I formed friendships quickly, usually telling everything I could about myself because I wanted so badly to be known. Most High School students didn't know what to do with all of my stuff, which made me even more insecure.

Some of my relationships proved to be more toxic than I knew. I was the rescuer — the fixer, right? My normal was to take on anyone's problems and make them better, no matter how badly it turned out for me.... and so I did.

---

[1] Normal. https://www.dictionary.com/browse/normal?s=t

[2] (Urban Dictionary is a crowdsourced online dictionary for slang words and phrases, operating under the motto "Define Your World."[2] The website was founded in 1999 by Aaron Peckham. Originally, Urban Dictionary was intended as a dictionary of slang, or cultural words or phrases, not typically found in standard dictionaries, but it is now used to define any word, event or phrase.)

[3] As I was researching "Yoke of Perfection" I came across several books, etc. One blog I found, had such a wonderful perspective on this issue of perfection. I share her page with you here: https://justasiam.ng/the-yoke-of-perfection/

[4] Yoke: https://www.merriam-webster.com/dictionary/yoke

[5] There is some good history and information in the following texts: Excerpt from The NLT Chronological Life Application Study Bible, New Testament Edition, (Tyndale Houses Publishers © 1996, 2004, 2015 by Tyndale House Foundation), pp. 1304. And an excerpt from The Word in Life Study Bible, New Testament Edition, (Thomas Nelson Publishers, Nashville; 1993), pp. 340-341.

[6] How we love those not like us is an issue that troubles me deeply in *The Church*, stemming from my passion for Him. My knowledge and understanding around socio economic barriers is limited, so writing about it here would not be wise. I know there are many books addressing these issues, but perhaps you have the capacity to write such a book. If you do, please consider sharing another perspective.

[7] Mirage. https://dictionary.cambridge.org/us/dictionary/english/mirage

Chapter 4

OH THE BLOOD OF JESUS

*"Oh precious is the flow
That makes me white as snow
No other fount I know
Nothing but the blood of Jesus"*[1]

Sitting in Grandma and Grandpa's living room with a gun held to my head I became keenly aware of my situation. Their home was empty except for me and an extremely desperate man.

I have to go back several years to explain what brought me to this moment…and how I victoriously walked away, but I can tell you this: had it not been for *The Church*, I may not have walked away.

THE TEEN YEARS

Struggle was the most consistent part of my young adult life. I was so insecure that I made myself vulnerable to everyone almost instantly. At the time, I couldn't tell you why. I didn't know what I was doing. I was just trying desperately to make an emotional connection somewhere. My neediness was repellent to a lot of people, but there were those who would prey on my vulnerability.

Once Dad got engaged, we started going to a new church and new schools. The moment we walked through the back doors of the new church I heard a sound that instantly won my heart. It was a gigantic youth choir singing with power and anointing. They were called "The Shekinah Singers". I was thrilled to learn that I was just the right age to join!

My solace and joy throughout these otherwise tumultuous years was singing with the Shekinah Singers. It was lead by a young couple that I also instantly loved and who are still part of my life this day, Jimmy and Johnna. They invested in the lives of so many, teaching us how to sing, how to dive deeper into worship and how to pray until we saw results. Jimmy and Johnna not only spent their time, they invested their lives into all of the young people, believing in and loving us.

While I loved singing in choir and being a part of the youth group, I was torn. I also wanted to be accepted and to "fit in" at school. It was almost as if I lived two lives. At school I was the new girl, so I dove into activities— basketball and school chorus — trying to make as many friends as possible. Most of the time I really was with fine being either place as long as I wasn't at home.

The home life was definitely inconsistent. My sister, my step brother and I lived in a constant state of guardedness. I mentioned some of my home turmoil in the last chapter but as I grew up, the home life continued to disintegrate. My dad and stepmom's rocky relationship put everyone in the house on edge, which caused her to lash out even more, in an effort to regain or maintain some of sort of control over life. Especially as a teenager, I received the words she spoke through the lens of her insecurities as bitter, mean and combative. Dad continued to work all the time. I knew that we needed money, yet all I could see was that he was slipping further away. I was losing him, losing his love.

Let me pause here and be clear: I don't blame anyone for the choices I made, but I also recognize that my "normal" was my compass. The enemy of my soul used the abandonment I experienced to twist my perspective. Even the words spoken over me during my teenage years: *"you're worthless, you could mess up anything, you're not feminine enough, no girl loves sports the way you do, are you gay, you were an accident"* — were seeds planted in my brain. After a while, I saw myself through that lens— unworthy of any good thing.

When I was 16-years-old, I began dating a boy, let's call him, Daniel. I knew Daniel quite well. We were friends, in fact, he had dated my best friend, Shawna, so the three of us spent a lot time together. I knew that Daniel and Shawna had been intimate. When they began having relationship trouble I intended to help salvage the relationship. However, becoming the go-between in order to fix them didn't work. In fact, it drove Daniel and me together. Inevitably they broke up and eventually Daniel and I began dating.

My feelings were euphoric. Someone saw worth in me. He seemed to genuinely care and to this day, I believe he did in the best way he knew how. His home life, his normal, was also dysfunctional, so we related to one another on many levels. We spent a lot of time together. He was handsome and very charming and my family liked him. The fact that he had been intimate with another girl didn't bother me. That was not going to happen with us. I was going to change him and save him and I was able to fight off his advances — for a while.

#didimentionthatihadabandonmentissues

One day, out of the blue, my dad and stepmom went on a trip and left the three of us kids with a family member. I was furious with my dad. He didn't tell us he was leaving. I remember that day well. The feelings of abandonment began to close in on me. I felt like I was drowning. In my teenage anger and disillusion, I did the only thing that made sense to me. I determined that I was going to "give in" to Daniel. He would be the man in my life from now on.

I snuck out of my house late that evening and a mutual friend of ours met me and drove me to Daniel's. Once it was all over, Daniel drove me home. Sneaking back in, undetected by anyone, I took a bath and went to bed. I remember thinking to myself at one point that night, *I am a 16 year old statistic*. It left me cold for one moment, but I quickly brushed that thought aside because I was in love! Everything was going to be alright!

The home life went from bad to worse. Eventually my dad and stepmom found out about my sleeping with Daniel. At that point I was on lock down. As long as I was living in my dad's home, I couldn't do anything, especially see or spend time with Daniel. Dad's disappointment in me was almost more than I could bear, but Daniel was still there for me. At least I could see him at school. I *needed* him.

I began talking with my mom about the whole situation on our occasional weekend visits. She offered me an option that I hadn't considered: I could move in with her and she would make plans to get me on birth control. So I did it. I moved in with my mom. The choice wasn't easy because I still battled the feeling that I needed to be there for my dad; but I wanted to live the way I wanted to live. Moving in with my mom was the answer. Church, the youth group, my friends, my family, my little sister, even my new baby brother, who was so precious — all went out the window over the love of Daniel.

Once I moved in with my mom it was no-holds barred on the relationship with him. At the same time he began being abusive and I just took it. He actually hit me quite often. One night on the steps of my mother's home, he choked me. I had chain prints on my neck and bruises from the jewelry I was wearing. I should have seen the signs, but I loved him, I had given myself to him and I thought to myself, *If I love him I'll stick with it and eventually he will change. I can love him out of this and then we'll live happily ever after.*

This went on for two more years. I'll spare you all of the details, but it got really hairy at the end. By this point I was in college. My grandparents lived close by so to save money I began living with them. They made a place for me — an apartment of sorts — in their basement where I could come and go. They were snowbirds who traveled to Florida on and off throughout the year, so on several occasions I had the entire house to myself.

LOVE IN ACTION

One evening when I was there alone, Debbie, my friend from church, called and began to talk to me about the Lord. She shared about the evangelist that spoke in church that night, about the Rapture[2] and how people who weren't walking with The Lord would be left behind. She said that she couldn't stop thinking about me. She pleaded with me to return to church and most of all, to return to Jesus. I told her I didn't know if I could. I really did miss church. I missed my relationship with the Lord most of all. I knew in my heart and mind that she was right, but I wasn't sure if I could walk away from the commitment I had made to Daniel.

> *And you must show mercy to those whose faith is wavering. Rescue others by snatching them from the flames of judgment. Show mercy to still others, but do so with great caution, hating the sins that contaminate their lives. —Jude 1:22-23*

Debbie persisted. Even though I didn't actually think I could or would go back to church, we prayed that night over the phone and something in me changed. I began praying again and I did start going back to church. Daniel could see the change in me too. I told him that we couldn't be intimate anymore, that I loved the Lord and I wanted to honor His will for my life. Part of honoring the Lord was cutting out intimate relations with Daniel until and unless we were married.

He, of course, didn't like it, but at first he did try to go along with my wishes. He had some understanding of church in his background, enough to know and understand where I was coming from. But it didn't last long. He began pressuring me again until it went to the point of date-rape. That's when I broke up with him.

I moved back to my dad and stepmom's house, broken and needing help. I have to tell you, they went to bat for me. My stepmom recognized the abusive situation. Daniel would call, not just once, but 10-15 times an hour. He would come by, he would threaten and she would call the police, call his parents and shield me from him as best she could. She understood what I needed.

My friends at church did their best to keep me occupied. We went to movies, to dinner, had game nights — whatever they could do so that I wouldn't return to that relationship that was destroying my life.

DANGER WILL ROBINSON!

One winter night while we were in church, Daniel came through the back doors into the foyer. He tried to get into the sanctuary and pull me out, but the security team somehow picked up on the situation and wouldn't let him in. They protected me while I was totally unaware of the entire situation. As he was leaving Daniel found and stole my coat so that I would have to come out and talk to him when church was over, but when I couldn't find my coat, the ushers redirected me. That was the night that I temporarily moved in with Natalie.

Natalie was a little older than me and much wiser in her faith-walk. She was single and she took me in. WHO DOES THAT? People who love The Lord and who put Him before the needs of themselves. I was a young woman in very serious need, yet she took me in, not only to protect me from Daniel, but even more, living with Natalie kept me from going back into a life-cycle that would have trapped me.

> **WHO IS WILL ROBINSON?**
>
> Will Robinson was a character from the 1965 SciFi television show called *Lost In Space*.[3] The series depicted an entire family, along with a friend, a doctor and a robot who were, as the title states, *Lost In Space*. Week after week the family faced new perils on new planets while trying to find their way home.
>
> The Robot — that was his name — served as young Will Robinson's best friend and guardian. Each time Will was about to face impending danger, The Robot's dryer vent arms would flail about, sternly repeating his warning, "Danger Will Robinson! Danger Will Robinson!" Will rarely heeded The Robot's admonition, even though The Robot always tried to keep him from walking into harmful situations.

Going to church all the time and living with Natalie was helping me grow in my relationship with the Lord. I asked her lots of questions about scripture and concepts that I had missed out on or didn't understand. I remember one night specifically asking her about the blood of Jesus. I had heard people when they prayed for me saying, "I plead the blood of Jesus." I had grown up in church the majority of my life, but I didn't understand that foundational truth.

She explained. "The blood of Jesus is the most powerful force on earth. Jesus gave his life so that we can know the Father. He gave Himself as the ultimate sacrifice. When people pray this way, they are asking that Jesus protect you with His blood. When we plead the blood of Jesus, we are asking for His protection over our lives, over situations that only He can change."

This was a new concept to me. I knew that Jesus' blood covered me and saved me from my sin, but I didn't know anything about pleading the blood — yet.[4]

I continued living with Natalie for a few short weeks. During that time, somehow Daniel found out where I was. Our three years together had our lives so intertwined that even his car title was in my name. He needed to renew his tags, so we planned to meet in order to get all of that straightened out. Knowing that all of that paperwork was at my grandparents' house we decided to meet there. He also knew that my grandparents were in Florida. That thought never crossed my mind. I just wanted to get it over with.

We met and entered the dark, quiet house. I went straight to the closet where the filing cabinet with important paperwork was kept. I was focused, digging for the car title and anything else that was keeping me tied to this relationship. Meanwhile, Daniel was looking for my grandfather's shotgun. He found it, loaded it and snuck up behind me. Feeling the barrel pressed into my temple, I froze. Daniel lead me to a chair in the living room.

"If you don't come back to me, I'm going to kill you." His eyes looked deranged. I began to shake as fear overwhelmed me. He was talking and spewing and crying all at the same time. "I can't live without you. I don't want to. I'll kill you then I will kill myself."

It was like an out of body experience for me but I knew he was serious. I was almost resigned that this was about to happen when my discussion with Natalie about the blood of Jesus popped into my head.

I began crying and praying aloud, "I plead the blood of Jesus. I plead the blood of Jesus."

He laughed. "If you think that's going to help you, you're wrong."

I continued, "I plead the blood of Jesus. I plead the blood of Jesus. I plead the blood of Jesus."

This went on for what seemed like an eternity. Me pleading the blood, him laughing and cursing. What seemed like hours ended abruptly, when all at once, he broke. He began bawling and saying he was sorry. He said he didn't know what had come over him. I told him he needed Jesus. I even prayed with him. Then I got out of there.

I was never again afraid of nor compelled to be with Daniel. It wasn't too long after that experience that I felt safe enough to leave Natalie's apartment and move back home. Daniel pulled a couple more incidents in an effort to win me back, including a suicide attempt. Thankfully they pumped his stomach and Daniel survived.

I moved forward and began walking more deeply in my relationship with Jesus.

IN THE MOMENT

None of this would have happened without people in *The Church* intervening.

> *My dear brothers and sisters, if someone among you wanders away from the truth and is brought back, you can be sure that whoever brings the sinner back from wandering will save that person from death and bring about the forgiveness of many sins.* —James 5:19-20

What if Debbie would have never called? What if she would have questioned herself: *Is this really the Lord telling me to call?* She could have thought in that moment, *I want to call Denise but I've got this to do. I'll call her later.* I have done that a thousand times. The thought comes to do good which is most often just outside my comfort zone. Yet Debbie didn't allow those thoughts to deter her.

She wasn't unkind or judgmental or shaming. She simply spoke the truth in love and invited me to walk a different direction. Her act of obedience began to literally change my path.

It is challenging to confront someone you love but it is the biblical thing to do.

> *Dear brothers and sisters, if another believer is overcome by some sin, you who are godly should gently and humbly help that person back onto the right path.* —Galatians 6:1

What if the ushers or security team at church would have ignored Daniel's intrusion in the middle of the service? They could have said to one another, "That's none of our business. We don't need to get involved." Instead, they intervened on behalf of a young woman who was walking her way back to the Lord. I don't know how they knew, but they were sensitive enough to hear His voice and obey.

> *Share each other's burdens, and in this way obey the law of Christ. If you think you are too important to help someone, you are only fooling yourself. You are not that important.* —Galatians 6:2-3

What if Natalie would have refused to take me in? She was young and single and had the right to live her own life at that moment, didn't she? As far I as I know Natalie never thought twice about taking me in. She even shared her own life with me, answering any questions and making sure that I was shielded from harm.

My heart is eternally grateful to these two women and even to my stepmom, who, though ours was one of the most difficult relationships in my life, recognized the signs of abuse and worked on my behalf to protect me.

> *Then these righteous ones will reply, "Lord, when did we ever see you hungry and feed you? Or thirsty and give you something to drink? Or a stranger and show you hospitality? Or naked and give you clothing? When did we ever see you sick or in prison and visit you?" And the King will say, "I tell you the truth, when you did it to one of the least of these my brothers and sisters, you were doing it to me!"* —Matthew 25:37-40

PLAY YOUR PART

Each person played a part in saving my life — literally. The Lord used them to draw me back to Him. I wasn't someone who was out of reach. I wasn't someone in a distant land. I was right there. I was already known by them, but they didn't think to themselves, *She's a lost cause. I'm wasting my breath. She'll never change.* They probably weren't even considering the above verse as they followed His heart. I believe they were simply doing the one thing Holy Spirit asked them to do, not knowing the outcome, not trying to figure it all out before they even began. I believe they were each simply being obedient in their faith walk.

How can the Lord use us this way? Are we willing to sacrifice time to make a phone call when He lays someone on our heart? Are we willing to say the hard stuff and risk being rejected? Are we willing to serve on a security team at our church that helps protect those around us? Are we willing, if the Lord asks, to give up space in our home? Could you or I take someone to dinner or a movie to keep them occupied while the Lord is doing a work in them?

Can the Lord break through someone's life without using people? There is no question that He can and sometime does, but He chooses to use us so that we can be in on what He is doing. We have the opportunity to witness Him in action, to use the gifts He's given us and to be a part of growing this body called *The Church*.

What is He asking of us so that we can be a viable living part of *The Church* — *The Church* that Jesus intended?

[1] Robert Lowry (1876). Nothing But the Blood of Jesus. Public Domain.

[2] The Rapture: Almost all evangelical Christians believe, according to Scripture that Jesus will return to rapture, or gather His bride. (1 Thessalonians 4:16) Though no one knows when (Matthew 24:36). If you don't know about or understand The Rapture, I recommend finding a study guide to walk you through the Bible, as well as reading books from reputable sources, such as Tipping Point by Jimmy Evans.

[3] Irwin Allen (Creator). (1965-1968); Lost In Space (Television Series). Burbank, CA: CBS https://www.imdb.com/title/tt0058824/?ref_=ttco_co_tt

[4] Jack Hayford says, "Pleading the blood of Jesus is not the superstitious application of a magic formula of words. Rather, a spiritual dynamic is being applied. The power of the blood of Jesus Christ is greater than both the energy of our own humanity and that of our Adversary. The power that saves is also the power that releases, delivers, and neutralizes the enterprises of hell and the weaknesses of the flesh. The appropriation of the power of the Blood in tough situations is intended for every believer in Christ to know, to understand, and to employ." https://www.jackhayford.org/teaching/articles/pleading-the-blood/

It also helps to understand our covenant with Jesus. He shed his blood for us on the cross. When we are in covenant relationship with Him, we have access to everything He is, including His blood and His authority.

Chapter 5

ABOUT THE BIRDS

PART 1 — PRESENT DAY

One Monday morning recently, exhausted after a wonderful weekend of worship, I knew I needed to rest. I asked the Lord, "How?" I know that sounds like a crazy question, but especially since I started my business several years ago, I really struggle at times to just "be". I feel like this is a struggle many of us face on a regular basis.

As I was fixing breakfast, the television show, "Family Affair" popped into my mind. I love that old show. I remember watching it when I was very young. I have re-watched it quite a bit since I discovered it on one of the streaming services a few years ago. Quite often the Lord has spoken to my heart through its simple episodes.

In case you've never heard of it, the show's main character is Uncle Bill, a wealthy New York bachelor. He gives up his bachelor lifestyle to adopt his nieces and nephew, whom he barely knows. Sadly, they lost their parents in a terrible car accident. Together, Uncle Bill and Mr. French, his gentleman's gentleman, take on the task of raising Sissy, his teenage niece, and Buffy and Jody, fraternal twins who are as curious as they are cute.

I turned on the television with the anticipation of relaxation and rest. The show is quite simple and emotionally non-taxing—my happy place!

In this episode[1], Buffy & Jody meet and adopt a Chinese grandfather, Grandfather Chang. Grandfather Chang lives with his son in New York City. However, Grandfather Chang is growing older and becoming very lonely. He is far away from his homeland and his own grandchildren are growing up and very busy. Grandfather Chang feels that he is no longer needed, even within his own family. On the flip side, Buffy and Jody have no living grandparents, so it is a perfect fit for the three.

When the children meet Grandfather Chang he takes them to his room where they discover he is surrounded by birds in cages. The children of course are curious, so Grandfather Chang explains that the birds are very important to him. With a gleam in his eye, he tells the children that when he was a boy in China he would often go along with his grandfather to walk their birds.

The children (and now I, staring at the television) offered a confused look about walking birds. It is an interesting word picture. One of the children even asks with a quizzical brow, "Do you put him on a leash?" My thoughts exactly, Buffy.

I thought about how hilarious it would look if I saw someone walking their bird — on a leash or even in a bird cage! No matter how hard I tried to imagine, bird walking didn't make sense to me.

Grandfather Chang further explained. An ancient custom of Chinese men was to keep and train birds. In this tradition, bird owners would train their birds to do amazing tricks and they indeed did walk the birds — in their cages, which allowed the birds to have some fresh air. The men would then hang the cages on low tree branches using the opportunity to socialize with one another.

I did a bit of research around the term "bird-walking". The hobby of bird keeping has been a famous tradition in China since the Qing Dynasty (1644 – 1911). For many, keeping birds was a way of passing the time. Most birds were well-trained. It was not uncommon to hear a myna belting out the entire Chinese National Anthem. While walking their birds, a bird's owner would swing the cage back and forth like a pendulum, forcing the bird to get off of it's perch and get a bit of exercise.[2]

WORD PICTURE

While I was finishing the episode, Holy Spirit spoke to my heart with a revelation. There are many people who are living like this. Like those birds in their cages, they have the feeling that they are free. It appears to them that they are out in the open, in their natural habitat. They are perched on a tree branch, in community with other birds, yet they are not really free.

This is how some of us are deceived.

Not free to fly, to build a nest, to hop around, to build relationship with other birds. In a TREE, yet still in a cage. The birds have the sensation of the wind in their feathers yet they are trapped. Deception. Some are tricked into singing songs that are not their natural song, through the approval and praise of man.

ABOUT THE BIRDS — PART 1

What is the price of two sparrows—one copper coin? But not a single sparrow can fall to the ground without your Father knowing it. And the very hairs on your head are all numbered. So don't be afraid; you are more valuable to God than a whole flock of sparrows. —Matthew 10:29

The one question that kept coming back to mind was this: Could we remain trapped in a prison because it's familiar or comfortable even though it's not safe?

This is a recipe for a life far from what God wants for His children.

Even if the cage door suddenly flung open, could we be so comfortable that we wouldn't walk or fly out? Fully embracing the freedom Jesus has for us?

Think about this: these Chinese bird cages, which are home to the birds, are very diverse and can be quite roomy. Some are gilded and ornate, some beautifully handcrafted out of bamboo. The cage floors are covered with elements from each bird's own natural habitat. Some have sand, some have dirt, all have perches — giving the bird the illusion that they are surrounded safely in their own environment — yet they are not free.

OUR MIND'S EYE

Several years ago we had a Shitzu named Samson. When we got him, we were told he was the runt of the litter. Either that wasn't true or we know how to love a dog well. He was so pleasant and grew to be strong and healthy. We attempted to crate-train him with a modicum of success, except for this one thing: if we left him in the very large crate with the door open, he wouldn't come out — even if we gently coaxed him or offered him a treat. Crying, yelping, barking to get out, he remained in his cage though the door was wide open, waiting on him to move forward.

The way was open. He could come and go as he

SIDE STORY

Timing is so interesting. Only the day before watching this episode I had been talking to my friend at church, J.D. He was sharing with me about how the Lord had used imagery from a movie to speak to his heart and reveal truth that morning in church. The Lord is so kind to do that for us—to speak to us through our everyday lives.

When we think about the Lord speaking to us, do we picture it like He spoke to Moses on Mt. Sinai? Do we think: *We're not ready, we don't have our stone tablets, we're unclean*? Yet often it is so simple. We just have to be listening.

We can't dismiss the ways He speaks. Jesus spoke to people in parables that related to their everyday lives. Those parables are still easily relatable, yet layered with truth. They are simple to receive, but as we grow in relationship with the Lord and His word, we continue to learn and understand their deeper meanings.

pleased — yet his mind told him he was trapped.

Thinking back to my own life, after my brush with a homicidal boyfriend, one would think that I would have gotten out of the cage. The door had been opened. I began moving closer to the exit yet I still didn't see myself as free. There was something that was holding me in the cage. It took several more years to completely break out.

[1] *Family Affair*, TV Series, Season 2, Episode 18. Writers: Don Fedderson, creator; Edmund Harmann, creator; John McGreevey, writer. https://www.imdb.com/title/tt0576802/fullcredits?ref_=tt_ov_wr#writers/

[2] http://www.culture-shock-tours.com/blog/going-for-a-walk-in-a-cage-10-facts-about-bird-keeping-in-china

MUSIC NOTES, CH 5: The song the Lord used to speak to J.D. that morning was *Defender*, one of my most favorite songs too. The imagery for him was a powerful picture from the old movie, *Gladiator*. It reminded J.D. that the Lord literally engages our enemy fiercely, even violently, in order to overwhelm him and give us amazing victory. I can't quote the specific lyric here, but if you listen to the song you will easily identify it and hopefully begin to understand how powerfully the Lord fights for you.

Find the by Gateway Worship version on YouTube at: https://youtu.be/wE1uEkWHHcI or in iTunes at: https://music.apple.com/us/album/defender-live/1430098208?i=1430099894

Songwriters: Steffany Dawn Gretzinger / John-Paul Gentile / Rita E. Springer
Defender lyrics © Bethel Music Publishing, Essential Music Publishing, Music Services, Inc

Chapter 6

LOVE OF ANOTHER KIND
PART 1

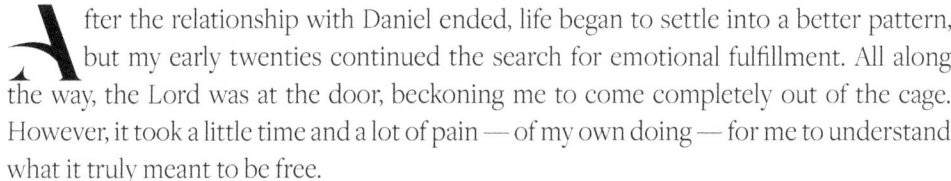

After the relationship with Daniel ended, life began to settle into a better pattern, but my early twenties continued the search for emotional fulfillment. All along the way, the Lord was at the door, beckoning me to come completely out of the cage. However, it took a little time and a lot of pain — of my own doing — for me to understand what it truly meant to be free.

MAKING CHANGES

My hometown college was a party college. I had definitely been a part of that scene during the Daniel years. My grades weren't great and I had no support system there. I knew I needed to change my surroundings, but I wasn't sure how to do that. I was already enrolled in college, actually because my dad worked at the school, I was going tuition-free, so I didn't see any way out that didn't seem wasteful. Lamenting all of this to my college advisor one afternoon, she asked me a question. "What is the one thing you would be doing right now if you could do anything?"

I replied, "Singing." It was a dream that I didn't think was possible, but she pointed out that if singing was my dream, now was the time to pursue it.

Becoming a rockstar wasn't the goal. My heart was to sing and lead worship in church. Music and worship had been the constants throughout my life. Leading worship was my heart's desire, but in those years, women weren't worship leaders or even pastors. At least not in our faith tradition. So, though I didn't know how it was going to work out or how I would even pay for it, I planned to go to a Christian college to purse a degree in music.

I lessened my full-time class load and began working and saving money. During this time I began dating David.

Actually, David and I grew up together, sort of. He, being four years younger than I, was never a blip on my romantic radar. I knew he was very talented and an anointed[1] musician, even from an early age, but to me he was just a good kid. For goodness sakes, when I got my driver's license, he was only 12. While I was in and out of church, struggling with relationships and trying like everything to find my way, David had grown into a fine young man.

At church, we were around one another a lot. We were both members of Shekinah Singers and as a choir and youth group, we traveled in packs, going out to eat and just hanging out. As only hindsight can teach, years later I learned that because he was so much younger than me it took him a minute to gather up the courage to ask me out.

When he finally asked, I politely (I think I was polite) said, "No, thank you." That was that.

I had been living way too "grown-up" to get involved with a kid. I didn't think twice about telling him no.

Relaying the whole scene to Debbie, her reaction wasn't what I expected. She told me that I needed to take another look at the young man. He wasn't a kid anymore. She encouraged me to reconsider. She hadn't lead me astray yet, so I listened to her.

Debbie and I cooked up a super-duper intricate plan so that she could let David know that I might be interested, after all. She literally said to him, "A little birdie told me that you should ask Denise out again. I think she'll have a different answer."

So he did and I said yes — but the rest is not happily-ever-after. He did ask and I did say yes… but then I decided I was right in the first place. David and I went out for maybe a week or two and then I called it off. Four months later at New Year's it was back on. Six months later it was off. Do you see a pattern? And because of the nature of our relationship — it was both emotional and physical — the final separation was an ugly break-up.

During those six months of dating, David told me that he had heard from the Lord and that I was the one he would marry. I wanted like everything to believe him, but I didn't. It wasn't long after this pronouncement that the final break-up occurred. During the breaking up process, he brought up God's plan again — the one where we were supposed to be married. At that point I smugly said to him, "When God tells me we'll both know."

God has a sense of humor and irony that is better than anyone. Ever.

But it would be a while before we got there. I remember telling some of my friends about David's "revelation" of our impending nuptials. We all had a good giggle. I moved on.

After the breakup, David and I both set off for college — the same college — at the same time. Inevitably we ran into one another. It's hard to get lost at a small, Christian college, though it does happen. We were both music majors, we were both new at the school and naturally, we crossed paths constantly.

In fact, the very first friend I met in a registration line at college was Rob. We hit it off instantly and I was so excited to have a new friend. Later that day I found out that Rob was David's roommate. Oh, the irony of the Lord.

There is so much to tell about those years. They were wonderful and I was maturing by leaps and bounds. I saw prayers, my prayers being answered and my needs being met. My school had financial help available. Everyday I got to sing — whether in choir or vocal lessons or practice. And on the weekends, my college choir, Campus Choir, traveled to other churches, singing and ministering the hope of Jesus to others. I discovered my love and passion and was finally beginning to find my sense of purpose.

Yet I still wasn't completely free from abandonment/codependent issues. I longed to have an emotional, personal connection with another human being. I went out on dates at college and none of those relationships went out of bounds. Though I was making great strides in my walk with Jesus, that yearning for connection drove many of my interactions with others. It was a constant gnawing in the back of my mind.

DREAMS COMING TRUE?

The summer before my second year at that college, I was doing a lot of reading and studying. I read the book "God's Smuggler" by Brother Andrew and my heart was on fire to share the Word with the underground church in Romania. I began praying about the wild possibility of going on a trip like that. I believed that anything was possible.

When school started back that fall, I traveled and sang with the choir almost every weekend. I loved every minute! Growing in my walk with the Lord and the confidence that brings, I became a section leader and the choir's public relations liaison for the school. I got to speak at churches often, promoting the school. Doc (Dr. David Horton) often introduced me to the congregation as "Jeremiah's Sister — the weeping prophetess". It was a joke, sort of. The truth is I was so grateful to be there and so filled with passion, I would cry every time I got up to speak, even if I was talking about the college!

I was tapped to participate in a small breakout group from the choir, Power Unlimited.

To my delight and astonishment the group was taking a trip to Romania that summer. Everything was falling into place. I felt like I was finally hitting my stride and becoming who I was meant to be. The funny thing is, even David was going to be a part of that small, traveling group. My dreams were coming true before my very eyes. Everything was on the precipice and then... I met someone.

> *"If you think you are standing strong, be careful not to fall."*
> *—1 Corinthians 10:12*

Without going into great detail, little by little the cage door seemed to begin closing. I found myself trapped again, but it was different this time. This time I was fully aware of my surroundings. I knew that the cage had enclosed me but I didn't see a way out. My secret relationship, which was unconventional to say the least, became public and I knew I would have to leave school. Shame played into every move I made.

Just like before, I was walking away from everything I held dear for the connection of another human. Even now, waves of emotion flood my heart as I think about those days.

This relationship rocked my Christian school world too. Doc, my mentor and spiritual father, came to my apartment along with many of my Campus Choir friends. They gathered around me as I was trying to pack my belongings.

He begged me to stay at school. He prayed with and for me. He promised that he and his wife, Virginia, would personally help me. He told me that the school had resources and counselors who could help me. My heart pounded at the overwhelming love and grace he was extending. I desired to stay yet I told him, "No." I almost couldn't believe the words that were coming out of my mouth. I loved this man with all my heart but I had made a commitment to this relationship and I was determined to follow through with it. So many commitments in my growing up years were broken. I was hell-bent on keeping this one.

There were so many other signs that I needed to escape from the cage, including an earlier campus visit from Dr. Jack Hayford, who spoke to the music department at large. He spoke specifically and pointedly to the entire group about unhealthy relationships. He had no idea who I was. There were 200-300 people in that room, yet somehow I knew he was talking directly to me. Still, I ignored every person and every sign, every voice that told me to turn around. I continued to pull the door closed, shutting out everyone and all my dreams.

> *The temptations in your life are no different from what others experience. And God is faithful. He will not allow the temptation to be more than you can stand. When you are tempted, he will show you a way out so that you can endure. —1 Corinthians 10:13*

But I didn't follow His way, His escape paths, plural.

I was at the height of where I wanted to be, my dreams for my life beginning to come true. Those dreams that God had placed in my heart from birth to only months before, those dreams that I was so passionate about — I relinquished, only to give in to my old patterns.

Embarrassed and ashamed, I determined to stay committed in a relationship that was not good or wholesome or healthy — or godly. In my mind it was as if I was the captain determined to sink with the ship.

That night, as I was carrying loads and packing them into the car David, my self-proclaimed, future husband showed up. He met me at the car. I'll never forget the seed he planted that night in obedience to The Lord.

"Denise — this isn't you."

The thing was, he wasn't trying to win me back or make the Word that God told him about us come true. In fact, I now know that he had come to grips with the fact that he had indeed heard the Lord. Most of us would say to ourselves, *We missed it. God didn't say that. I misheard or it was the pizza I'd eaten the night before.* No, David knew that he had heard The Lord, but he also knew that I had stepped away from God's will for my life. There was nothing he could do about that. Where our relationship was concerned, it was over. He had moved on.

Yet he stopped by that night to tell me that I didn't belong in the situation I had found myself in. He knew it, everyone around us knew it, except for me. *I'm getting what I deserve*, were my thoughts. *I'm losing everything, but I can take it.*

I did leave. The school made their choice by inviting me to leave. I made my choice too.

BACK TO OHIO

I went back to Ohio. Also the words of a song written by Chrissie Hynde[2] that come to my mind every time I think about that trip. In her song, Chrissie talks about going back home and everything in the city had changed — from good to bad. Everything changed for me too. From bad to worse.

My friend, Jamie, moved back to Ohio with me in order to pursue our relationship. We temporarily moved in with my mom. It was the one place I knew that she and I could live any way we wanted. Mom saw it as an opportunity to keep her daughter safe and from living in the streets.

I had a sweet, baby sister who was now-five-years old. Amber was one of my greatest joys during this season, but at the same time, I was either with Amber or with my friend. I had no moments alone. No time to think. No time to myself. I tried to start journaling again. I bought a new book with empty pages and waited.

> **Journal Entry:** *"May 8 ... was the first day I was going to write in my book — but I couldn't quite get a moment to myself — quite like now."*

Happiness evaded me even though I was living on my so-called principles of commitment at any cost. Friends would call or send letters now and then. Some were helpful. Some were not. I remember receiving a letter that I perceived as condemnation from a college sweetheart. We were very close friends, but it never blossomed into anything more. In his mind, he was trying to help me break free. What I heard through his words were echoes of my past and confirmation of the words spoken over me years before: *you're worthless, you could mess up anything, you're not feminine enough, no girl loves sports the way you do, are you gay, you were an accident.*

So, I worked. I came home. I played with my little sister and I prayed. I didn't even know if God could hear me, I felt so far away — but that didn't stop me from trying. I remember quietly asking the Lord to help me get out of this situation. I had no idea how that was going to happen. I kept trying to journal. Journaling was the one thing that was all mine.

> **Journal Entry:** *"May 15 ... It's raining— I love the rain— I wish it would rain in me. The storm is brewing, but there's still a ways to go before the clouds burst and release the sweet peaceful rain.*
>
> *I hate the devil. Every time I get a moment to myself to even begin to talk about my feelings, someone comes around. Today it's my baby sister.*
>
> *I thought maybe on my day off I could have a few hours to myself. You see, the devil knows that if I don't, I will die. So, he stops me every chance I get. Like now. The phone is ringing. It's for me. Jamie will be home in less than an hour.*
>
> *So many things are confusing in my life. So many pressures, so many people want so many different things from me. I've been here before — but somehow this time things have changed. Pressures are harder — maybe not. Maybe I just don't remember. Yet it seems there is so much more at stake.*
>
> *Writing has always been my outlet. When I stopped, I just kept it all inside of me until it was too late. So this time I shall bare all — to You, Lord. This is for You and me and hopefully, before long, I can begin having real conversations with You again. I miss You, my Lord. I long*

for the time You will again take charge of my life. I dream at night of all the possibilities You have in store for me.

I knew "the fall" was coming. Somehow I just knew it, but I couldn't stop, I couldn't keep it from coming about. I didn't know how to fight for myself. I thought I was too strong to need or burden anyone else.

I've been so wrong. I want to change things, but I don't know how — I mean, I do, but it's so hard...

... Please let this fall make me stronger, Lord. I've already realized a few things on my own. Simple wisdom, yet it takes real knowledge...

Hopefully, eventually I can go deep inside my innermost being and You can begin the healing process within me — not me — You. I can do nothing on my own.

Lord, please help me out of this predicament. I love my friend so much... in the right way and I must admit to myself — I must make myself admit that I love ... in the wrong way. It's not on purpose. It has only developed since, "the fall". It was all so perfectly innocent.

.... I'm going to have to close for now. I don't want anyone to know about my writings just yet. I do love You, Lord. I do love You. Please help me."

BACK TO LIFE

Within less than 2-weeks of that journal entry, out of the blue, David called. He invited me to come to church and just like the first time he asked me out, I told him no, but he was very persuasive. Power Unlimited would be singing at my home church and he insisted that everyone in the group — all the people I left behind, including Doc — wanted to see me. It wasn't a long conversation. Yet he called me — this young woman who had broken his heart and derailed his life-plan — to invite me to church. Once again, he was being obedient to Lord with no thought of romantic connections — no strings attached.

This slowly opening door seemed to be the opportunity I had been longing for and writing about in my journal. Even though the self-inflicted shame I felt was almost overwhelming, I loved those people with all my heart. The internal struggle over whether or not to go to church was fierce but I opted to go.

That night my life changed forever.

As Power Unlimited sang, my protective shell began to crack. Doc began talking about the love and grace of God and I almost couldn't sit still. Heart pounding and hot tears streaming down my face, I took a step. As Doc asked for anyone who wanted to come to the altar and pray, I got out of my seat and began making my way to the front of the church. I was barely able to stand as overwhelming grace met me there standing in front of Doc. Before I knew it, I was surrounded. It was beginning to rain.

Everyone in the group as well as my church people gathered around and prayed with me and for me. The spirit of God spoke to my heart. Though I still didn't see how, deep down inside I was peace-filled for the first time in a long time. I had hope that God still loved me and wanted to have a relationship — with me.

I will always remember that night with a grateful heart. I had what Doc called, "a watershed moment."[3] I didn't even know what that was. All I knew was that those prayers I prayed when I wasn't "living right", those prayers in my journal crying out the Lord for help, were being answered.

> *I waited patiently for the LORD to help me,*
> *and he turned to me and heard my cry.*
> *He lifted me out of the pit of despair, out of the mud and the mire.*
> *He set my feet on solid ground and steadied me as I walked along.*
> *He has given me a new song to sing, a hymn of praise to our God.*
> *Many will see what he has done and be amazed.*
> *They will put their trust in the LORD.*
> *—Psalm 40:1-3*

After church we all went to eat together. Being with PU (our affection acronym for the group) was like home to me. They could have judged me. They could have said they didn't want anything to do with me, but they didn't. They were a part of loving me back to Jesus.

Within another week, my friend moved out. There was no conversation about it at all. Jamie was homesick and decided to leave. It was an answer to prayer that made a hard conversation much easier for me. God intervened.

AFTER THE RAIN

Looking back, I marvel at how Doc showed Jesus' love to me.

More than coming by that fateful move-out day (along with many members from the choir) he began by telling me the truth in love about where I found myself and prayed with me —that day. He went out on a limb by offering to help me find counseling, acting as an advocate with the school and surrounding me with support. All of this, he gave out of his own time and his own life with no personal gain. Thank God it wasn't the last opportunity I had to be mentored by Doc.

> *And you must show mercy to those whose faith is wavering...*
> *—Jude 1:22*

And what an example his love in action was for the many choir members who came to my apartment that day? It wasn't just for me — Jesus' love through Doc's actions showed a group of young men and women how to show Jesus' love in deed to those in crisis.

Years later I learned that during that season, Doc told the choir during a prayer meeting, "Sin is sin. Either we serve a God who can forgive and restore or we don't." That statement locked in David's personal theology for the rest of his life. Either God can forgive sin or He can't.

Years later, I realized that much of what I perceived about grace wasn't quite right, though the Lord still used what I did understand to lead me back to Him. For instance, I learned that it is harder to "backslide"[4] than I thought. We are human. We will mess up. We will sin. It isn't one sin that caused me to begin to lose relationship with the Lord. It was a heart of pride that put the distance between us, separating us. If I went on living the way I wanted, willfully walking in the opposite direction of Him, knowing that I was living outside of His will for my life, but not caring, I was the one pushing Him away. He was never far. It was I who went deeper and deeper into the cage.

TRUTH BE TOLD

I've known many, myself included, who grew up in church with the perception that The Lord is not listening if we aren't living perfectly. What a load and a lie from the pit?!

The Lord is ever near, ever wanting to have a relationship with us. He understands that we are not perfect (Psalm 103:14), yet He chooses us to be His people and He chooses to use us to reach people — in spite of — I would dare even say because we struggle.

Our weakness shows off His strength.

Each time he said, "My grace is all you need. My power works best in weakness." So now I am glad to boast about my weaknesses, so that the power of Christ can work through me.
—2 Corinthians 12:9

> *So we must listen very carefully to the truth we have heard, or we may drift away from it. —Hebrews 2:1*

Even now my heart aches a little at what I missed when I walked away from college. I think about how differently life could have been. More than likely David and I would have mended our relationship just by our being a part of Power Unlimited, but I was broken. I needed healing. I had to come to the end of my emotional bondage.

God heard my prayers and helped me begin to set things right. Even if I hadn't gone to that church service, He would still be chasing me. That is how great the Father's love remains.

I began the journey to restoration that night in 1990. I started going back to church and getting involved. This is where "My Tribe" comes in.

---

[1]*"To be anointed is to be set apart, empowered, or protected."*
https://www.crosswalk.com/faith/bible-study/what-does-it-mean-to-be-anointed.html

[2]*Songwriters: Christine Hynde / Dave Brock / N. Turner ©1982*
My City Was Gone lyrics © Sony/ATV Music Publishing LLC

[3]*Watershed Moment, Figurative meaning: A watershed moment is a turning point, the exact moment that changes the direction of an activity or situation. A watershed moment is a dividing point, from which things will never be the same. It is considered momentous, though a watershed moment is often recognized in hindsight. https://www.verbling.com/discussion/idioms-watershed-moment#:~:text=A%20watershed%20moment%20is%20a,is%20often%20recognized%20in%20hindsight. Accessed 04/26/25*

[4]*Backslide: 1: to lapse morally or in the practice of religion; 2: to revert to a worse condition.*
"Backslide." Merriam-Webster.com Dictionary, Merriam-Webster, https://www.merriam-webster.com/dictionary/backslide. Accessed 23 Sep. 2020.

Chapter 7

MY TRIBE

... So they dug a hole through the roof above his head. Then they lowered the man on his mat, right down in front of Jesus. —Mark 2:4

PRESENT DAY

Wow. My Pastor preached a sermon that really brought this scripture alive in me. If you read this passage in context, it's not clear if these men asked permission to dig through another man's roof — but what is clear is that there was *no other way*. They knew they had to get their friend to Jesus.

They vandalized a home — broke protocol — to get this man in front of the only One that could help him. Do you know what those roofs were made from? Mud, straw, clay and manure. They dug through that nastiness and lowered their friend into the room, probably reaching through the muck with bare arms and hands to do so. They didn't have cranes. They probably didn't have a hoisting mechanism, yet they did the unthinkable. They risked everything, including paying for roof repairs, becoming stinky and icky and facing possible arrest.

In the words of P.G. (Pastor Gary Satterly): "To reach people no one else is reaching, we're going to have to do things no one else is doing."

The four men got personally involved. They stopped whatever they were doing. They interrupted their lives because they *knew* what Jesus could do. There was no other way. These men didn't merely tell their paralytic friend, "We'll pray for you." They invested everything to make sure he got to Jesus.

UNLIKELY GRACE

"The only thing worse than being lost is being lost and no one is looking for you." P.G.

WALKING TOWARDS THE CAGE DOOR

I think back to the time I was coming out of the cage — coming back to life, so to speak. I had several mentors along the way. There was one who called to check on me almost daily during this season. She made it clear that I could call on her any time of the day or night. Her name is Johnna. You might remember her from a few chapters ago. In that season of my life Johnna was Jesus with skin on— loving me like Jesus loved.

We had many, many long conversations. I was so needy, yet she took time out of her days, night and life to give me counsel, prayer and encouragement. Johnna wasn't calling me to get the scoop or tell me, "Praying for you," then hang up the phone. She got down in my muck with me. She didn't just say she loved me. She loved me in deed (1 John 3:17). She didn't candy coat the things I needed to hear. She wasn't mean. She wasn't harsh. Johnna met me with grace then told me the truth, making sure I got to Jesus.

I'm not sure if Johnna realized it when she gave me this verse to cling to, but it has been one of my life verses. Luke 22:31-32:

> *"Simon, Simon, Satan has asked to sift each of you like wheat. But I have pleaded in prayer for you, Simon, that your faith should not fail. So when you have repented and turned to me again, strengthen your brothers."*

On a late night phone conversation, Johnna spoke this into my life with such wisdom. It resonated in my heart. Dare I believe that Jesus was interceding for me? Dare I believe that someday I could be restored and live out His mission for me? To be honest, at that moment I didn't believe it. I didn't feel worthy of serving the Lord in any way, yet I had hope that there was still a plan for my life. She continued to talk to me, day after day, night after night for that season. I wasn't completely out of the cage yet. It was literally a fight every day.

My mind waged a war in me. I grappled with loss and with feeling lost. I knew I was forgiven, but I still really wrestled

SIDE STORY

I still tease Johnna and her twin sister, Wanda, (whom I talk about in another chapter) that my WWJD bracelet was actually WWWJD for What Would Wanda or Johnna Do? I don't mean that to be irreverent, but each of them influenced my life in considerable ways.

One of the most impactful gifts they have in common is the easy way they share about the Lord. When either of them got up to speak, they used examples from everyday life or powerful word pictures that made the truth of scripture come alive.

with guilt. And because I didn't yet fully understand grace, I didn't think I could ever get back to the life I dreamed of. I judged that person in the mirror every day.

So I prayed as much as I could. I wrote — a lot. I hung scripture on that mirror, on my door, beside the light switch, even on the wall by my bed so it would be the first thing I saw when I opened my eyes. Johnna walked that portion of the path with me — all the way. *All the way.*

I knew she was praying — she prayed *with* me. She invested her time, her wisdom and her experience. It wasn't like she didn't have anything to do. Besides taking care of her family, she was teaching at a school in town, co-leading a choir and more. I'm sure spending time with me was not convenient for her, but she listened to and obeyed the Lord and helped get me to Jesus. She dug deeply through that roof, a few times, as my healing progressed.

Have you ever done that for anyone? I don't suggest it unless you know that The Lord is leading you there. That's one of the things that got me into trouble in the first place.[2] I thought it was my job in life to deliver people, but I didn't know how. Instead of getting people to Jesus, I ended up taking on their issues when I hadn't dealt with my own.

THERE WERE MORE
Johnna wasn't the only one. Debbie was there ... and so was Carla and Sharon and Dennis and Naomi and Theresa and Jody and Wanda and .... to be honest, most of them could care less about being named. In fact, there is no way to name them all because while the above were with me on a regular basis, many others were there at the right moment, speaking life to me, encouraging me or praying for me. Each one is a part of my life and my story and are forever in my heart.

At the time I didn't own a car, so collectively or one at time, they picked me up and took me places. We went out to dinner, to movies and to one another's houses to play games or just have fun. We didn't always have deep conversations, though we did sometimes, but these people of God got me out of the house, away from being alone and into healthy situations that began to make me feel like I was a part of something — I belonged — and it was healthy!

They kept a watchful eye on me. They prayed for me. Sometimes they would have to talk me into going to church functions because there were moments when shame got the best of me and tried to keep me away. Notes of encouragement often found me at the moment I needed them.

While I was moving towards freedom, my choir director, Jimmy, wrote me short encouraging notes that I still have to this day because those simple words helped convince me that I could make it.

After my healing process was well underway I began singing in the choir again. Jimmy and Johnna didn't banish me to a corner for punishment. They walked the journey with me and when they sensed I was ready to come back, they welcomed me with open arms. I became a functioning part of the body again. I was coming back to life, growing stronger in a healthy place.

The Lord used people to give Scripture, speak truth, even sing songs at just the right moment to keep me pointed in the right direction. One song I have never forgotten was a simple song taught to me by one of the church pastors. One that he learned as a child. Though it seemed elementary at the time, it has stuck with me all these years:

> *I'm a child of God, I'll have no fear,*
> *He has chosen me to win,*
> *I am known as friend to the Great I Am,*
> *I'm a child of God!*[1]

Simple, yet life changing. I can't tell you how many times when I was at my lowest, fighting shame and fear and feeling like I would never be completely free, this little song would pop into my mind. There were and are still many moments when I declare this at the top of my lungs.

These acts of obedience, love and grace and many more from the people the Lord put in my life during that season are still a part of me.

SIN NO MORE

It wasn't a perfect process, in fact, it was messy. I was in the struggle, yet the people who were *The Church* got in there with me. I was still walking out some of the hardest days of my life. I had issues. I was needy. I'm sure it wasn't always easy for people to "speak the truth in love" to me.

> *Dear brothers and sisters, if another believer is overcome by some sin, you who are godly should gently and humbly help that person back onto the right path. And be careful not to fall into the same temptation yourself. Share each other's burdens, and in this way obey the law of Christ. If you think you are too important to help someone, you are only fooling yourself. You are not that important.* —Galatians 6:1-3

But each week it got easier. Each day I had something to look forward to. I was accepted even though I was a mess. I had pastors who knew the way I had lived and they loved me still. They weren't afraid of what anyone else thought as far as I knew and still know. They just knew I needed to know the love of Jesus. They knew I still struggled, but they loved me anyway and brought me alongside to learn and grow in my walk with Jesus.

One hazard of our "microwave" society has been the expectation that things — and people — should be done quickly. If I hadn't been given the space to process or time to grow while coming out of my struggles, I may never have understood the fullness of God's grace. If I hadn't been allowed to exercise my faith with grace, I may never have stayed.

What if I would never have been allowed to walk past the shame that tried to hold me back?

I'm thinking about the woman who was caught in an adulterous affair in John chapter eight (John 8:1-11).[3] The teachers of religious law and the Pharisees, stones in hand, drug her in front of the whole church crowd while Jesus was teaching. They were ready to execute punishment according to the letter of the law. Jesus turned everything around.

"All right, but let the one who has never sinned throw the first stone!" In my imagination I hear Him say, "Drop your rocks!" I sometimes think I would have loved to know what Jesus was writing in the sand, but then again, what if He were writing my name or my sins there?[4] Even the deceived religious leaders knew that they were not without sin. If you don't know the story, please stop right now and read it.

After the men walked away, Jesus took it even further, saying to the woman, "Where are your accusers? Didn't even one of them condemn you?"

"No, Lord," she said.

And Jesus said, "Neither do I. Go and sin no more."

What did that mean? Did He mean that she would have to live so perfectly that she would never sin again? And if she did sin, how would she ever recover? How could anyone live that life?

I surmise that when Jesus was telling this woman go and sin no more, He was saying, "Don't go back into this sinful lifestyle. Don't choose to go back to what you know. I love you. This is a life-changing moment. Keep moving forward with Me. You will get past this."

Jesus disarmed her shame.

My pastors at that time in my life did that for me. Pastor Timmerman and his wife, Momma Jan did life with me and spoke truth to me many times over. One truth he spoke shifted my entire perspective about sin from that day forward.

He said, "During this process, you're going to take some steps backwards, but it's okay. Just don't go all the way back, keep moving forward, keep moving towards Jesus."

Keep moving towards "The Door," John 10:7, NKJV.

Though I desperately wanted to, I couldn't change all at once. I needed to walk through the healing process with the help of others that God place in my life. Sometimes that's how it is supposed to be.

> **SIDE NOTE**
>
> During one of my many conversations with Momma Jan, she was sharing with me how she prayed, every day.
>
> She said, "Denise, I ask the Holy Spirit to be involved in every thought, every word I speak, every detail of my day, every day."
>
> I was amazed because I thought surely she didn't need to ask for that kind of help anymore. To me, she was nearly perfect.
>
> But, oh how precious that prayer has become in *my* every day.

*Put on your new nature, and be **renewed** as you learn to know your Creator and become like him. —Colossians 3:10*

LIVING WATER

One night during that season, Pastor Timmerman preached on Living Water.

> *On the last day, that great day of the feast, Jesus stood and cried out, saying, "If anyone thirsts, let him come to Me and drink. He who believes in Me, as the Scripture has said, out of his heart will flow rivers of living water." But this He spoke concerning the Spirit, whom those believing in Him would receive; for the Holy Spirit was not yet given, because Jesus was not yet glorified... —John 7:37-39 NKJV*

Pastor was well into his sermon when all at once, I began to cry out — a loud, guttural cry. I was tuned in to the Word he was speaking yet I couldn't stop. I was being filled with Living Water that very moment. The weird thing was, I wasn't embarrassed or afraid at all. It was as if the Lord was using me to prove His point but at the same time, freeing me of so many of the weights I carried. Pardon my saying it this way, but it was like I was throwing up — vomiting the past and allowing the fresh Living Water to renew me. I mean, this was in front of the whole church and no one stopped me. No one called me out or said I was being a distraction.

In fact, I remember Pastor addressing this event while he was preaching. "That is living water flowing out of Denise." Something like that. All I knew is that something was happening. Something was changing in me. The Lord was doing a work inside of me in front of the whole church. On purpose.

Looking back, I wonder if it was two-fold? The way the Lord operates is mind-blowing. He accomplishes His purpose in and through us if we allow Him access. That night, I wonder if he was showing the body that a life surrendered to Him and surrounded by fellow believers could indeed be changed?

It was a wonderful night. By the end of the sermon people had surrounded me and were praying for me. The load that was lifted off of my life that night was more than I know how to tell you, but it was real.

So, I continued to walk with my people. My tribe as we like to say. We all grew together.

> *Let us hold tightly without wavering to the hope we affirm, for God can be trusted to keep his promise. Let us think of ways to motivate one another to acts of love and good works. —Hebrews 10:23-24*

KOINΩN'IĄ (KOINONIA)

The Lord uses whomever is willing. Sometimes He works through old friends or perhaps, new friends, even people we barely know. Often He uses a pastor or maybe another leader in the church: but what if He wants to use you or me? Maybe you don't hold any role in the church or even go to church, but you know Jesus and you hear His voice.

Being "used" by the Lord sounds ominous, but all it really means is that we embrace and carry out His nudging. Anyone can send a note. It's a lot easier these days. It's called a text message, but hand-written notes seriously can't be beat. Maybe you're supposed to spend some time with someone and just listen. Maybe you're a part of the group who can take that person to dinner or to a movie, to a HEALTHY place, just to show them the love of Jesus. One time, the group took me to see *Footloose*. Who'd have thought Jesus could use *Footloose*? But He did.

> *And let us not neglect our meeting together, as some people do, but encourage one another, especially now that the day of his return is drawing near. —Hebrews 10:25*

In the early church it was called fellowship. Not the catch-all phrase "fellowship" that we church-folk use to describe social interactions. I'm talking about truly investing in, participating in and partnering with others to make sure we are all connected to Jesus and through Him connected to one another. The early church set the standard for living in fellowship.

> *All the believers devoted themselves to the apostles' teaching, and to fellowship, and to sharing in meals (including the Lord's Supper), and to prayer.* —Acts 2:42

The word fellowship here comes from the Greek word, Koinonia. While there is no one word in English that captures the entire scope of what Koinonia means, the word fellowship is often used as the translation in a variety of contexts. In my studies I've learned that Koinonia in the verse above means: partnership.[5]

That speaks to so much more than greeting one another in church or a having potluck dinner as being fellowship. It means getting involved, thinking about someone else's needs above our own, extending grace that points to Jesus.

And even though I was met with such sweet grace, I cannot say that I have always extended this grace.

CONFESSIONS FROM SOMEONE WHO FORGOT

I have to confess right here that there have been moments where I have looked at someone that God placed in my path, someone who needed an investment of time or a gesture of kindness and thought to myself, *I don't have time for this.*

When I first met Mikey, I wanted to just put him aside. He was such a needy kid. You could just feel it in the way he talked and hung around my desk at work. I didn't have time. I had just lost my career, sent my son off to his freshman year of college, had all of the duties in my role at church and was starting a business. I was graciously gifted with a job a at a friend's business during this time, which is where I met Mikey, but I didn't have time for another "project". Seriously, I just wanted the kid to go away... but the Lord, and my sweet husband, began dealing with my heart.

My husband knew a little more about Mikey's situation than I did and he told me that Mikey was in a very vulnerable place. There had been a time in Mikey's short life where he had little to no parental support and that possibly he was trying to find himself. David gently pointed out that Mikey needed strong Christians in his life. He suggested that I take a pause and really ask The Lord what my role should be. I am so glad that I listened and did as David advised.

For the first time in a long time I began focusing on someone other than me. Not only that, but Mikey soaked up everything I said like a sponge. He had so many questions! We talked about The Lord a lot but he also confided in me and asked for advice about life and what his response should be in certain situations. My heart started to turn towards him and I realized that this was an opportunity for me to pour into a kid's life the way someone poured into mine.

I was being *The Church* — outside of the four walls — just like my tribe was *The Church* for me.

Mikey had other influences too. His uncle and aunt were able do life with him, watching movies, having dinner and conversation. Mikey started going to our church and my husband gave him a way to start playing in the worship band. The whole choir adopted him and his girlfriend, Sophie. As far as I know, they have never left their tribe.

I wonder if Johnna was ever tempted to push me aside just like I wanted to ignore Mikey? It is easy for us to do. Life is busy. Things happen. It can be hard and uncomfortable and messy to line someone's exit path to The Door. But He doesn't ask one of us to do it ALL. He asks each of us, with such grace, to follow Him, using the gifts He's given us.

> *Just as our bodies have many parts and each part has a special function, so it is with Christ's body. We are many parts of one body, and we all belong to each other. In his grace, God has given us different gifts for doing certain things well. So if God has given you the ability to prophesy, speak out with as much faith as God has given you. If your gift is serving others, serve them well. If you are a teacher, teach well. If your gift is to encourage others, be encouraging. If it is giving, give generously. If God has given you leadership ability, take the responsibility seriously. And if you have a gift for showing kindness to others, do it gladly.* **Don't just pretend to love others. Really love them**. *Hate what is wrong. Hold tightly to what is good. Love each other with genuine affection, and take delight in honoring each other.*
> —Romans 12:4-10

All I had to do with Mikey was make a small investment. Those investments don't come with a guarantee, yet we are called to be obedient. To love without reservation. To get involved with people and to get them to Jesus.

My tribe didn't bring up charges against me in front of the church or to Jesus. My tribe tore the roof off in order to get me to Him. The Lord used them as a part of the process while He did a work in me, peeling away the layers of my shame, abandonment and recklessness until I allowed the only One I needed to be the only One who met my need. My deepest felt need — to be known — was met by a loving God who surrounded me with loving people — *The Church*.

In order for us to do what my tribe did for me, sometimes we'll have to think outside of the box. We may to have dig through a roof to help someone break through, but if we can get people to Jesus, He will do the rest. His love changes everything.

During this time over 30 years ago, that love took hold of my life. It's a different kind of love. A love that continues to change me still today.

[1] *Author Unknown*

[2] *Codependency — The word is used so much that it has almost become a "buzzword" but the issue is as prevalent as ever. Especially as Christians, we can misunderstand our responsibility to love and care for others and can take it to an extreme that the Lord never intended. If you are codependent with another person, it means that your emotional and psychological state overly relies on him or her. While it's good to care for, help and support people, the codependent person crosses a line in the relationship. I have seen codependent relationships that developed into an unhealthy soul-tie.*

None of those who walked this out with me made it about themselves or allowed me to make it about them. They consistently pointed me to Jesus. He did the rest. Though they were with me through that intense season, we don't get to spend very much time together now. Life has taken us different directions and sometimes to different states. But when we have the opportunity to see one another, it's as if we haven't lost a minute. That's something only the love of Jesus can do.

[3] *Throughout the book I give multiple scripture references and ask for you to read it for yourself. If you don't have a Bible or access to a Bible, I highly recommend the YouVersion Bible App. It's free! There are many different versions of the Bible to choose from which you can download to your phone or tablet and there are many Bible studies within the App itself. Find it at: https://www.youversion.com/. Another App I use is Bible Hub, also free, also loaded with different versions, but an added bonus is access to Bible commentaries, Strong's Concordance and the Interlinear Bible, which sentence structures in Greek and Hebrew. Find it at https://biblehub.com/.*

[4] *Since writing this, I have thought about the statement I made here: "...what if He were writing my name or my sins there?" Writing in the dust was a common practice in that day when teaching. I don't know what He wrote that day. Some commentaries assert that Jesus wrote the sins of the accusers. In my mind, that would make Him an accuser and Jesus is not our accuser Maybe it was a list of sins, without naming the accuser. I don't know if it was what He wrote; but what He said was, "All right, but let the one who has never sinned throw the first stone!"*

[5] *From Strong's Lexicon: koinonos; partnership, i.e. participation, or intercourse, or benefaction. https://biblehub.com/greek/2842.htm*

Chapter 8

LOVE OF ANOTHER KIND
PART 2

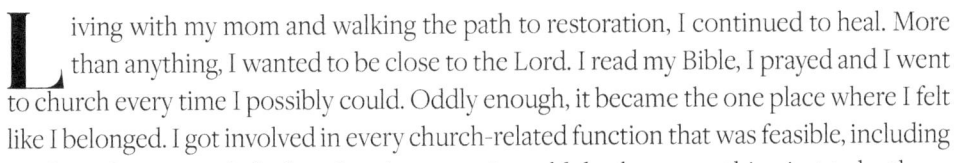

Living with my mom and walking the path to restoration, I continued to heal. More than anything, I wanted to be close to the Lord. I read my Bible, I prayed and I went to church every time I possibly could. Oddly enough, it became the one place where I felt like I belonged. I got involved in every church-related function that was feasible, including working the janitor shift after church events. I would do almost anything just to be there.

The Associate Pastor would open every service at church with scripture and prayer. One particular night he gave me my sword and shield for the next leg of my journey:

> *I have been crucified with Christ; it is no longer I who live, but Christ lives in me; and the life which I now live in the flesh I live by faith in the Son of God, who loved me and gave Himself for me. —Galatians 2:20 NKJV*

> *Therefore, if anyone is in Christ, he is a new creation; old things have passed away; behold, all things have become new.*
> *—2 Corinthians 5:17 NKJV*

With gratitude I often think about that night, remembering it like it was yesterday. I can tell you exactly where I was sitting when I underlined those verses in my Bible.

I sometimes wonder if, as the Associate Pastor planned what scripture he would use that night, he thought to himself, *These verses are too familiar.... why don't I go with something else?* I'm sure the Lord would have shown me these verses another way, but the Lord used him. Perhaps it wasn't even a question for him, but I'm so glad he chose to open the service that night with those passages.

I think about these things often because I know that I still have moments when I second guess something the Lord is telling me to do, even in small things. Yet these two verses, Galatians 2:20 and 2 Corinthians 5:17 were transformational. I clung to them for dear life. They spoke over me, to me, around me and through me. I dared to believe that I could be made new!

There was a song that I listened to over and over during this season. *Change Your Nature* (thank you Bebe Winans) ministered truth to me and brought home the point of the two life-giving verses given to me by that precious Associate Pastor.

The Lord was indeed changing my very nature. Filled with hope, I kept moving forward, doing the only things I knew to do. Going to church, listening to christian music and radio, attending church functions, prayer meetings, talking with my tribe and even on occasion, watching christian television. I must admit there have been many times when "Christian Television" seemed to be an oxymoron, yet the Lord used it to speak to me. There were programs and people on christian television and radio who were and are a part of *The Church* that were instrumental in my healing process.

BREAKING GOOD

One afternoon Mom and I were doing some things around the house, listening to Christian television. There was a couple being interviewed about how they broke ties with their past relationships. This piqued my interest, so I sat down and watched. I don't remember everything they said, but I do remember they talked about breaking soul ties with previous relationships. I didn't even know what that was. As I watched, I quickly learned that it had to do with severing bonds where there had been an emotional connection to another person, including but not limited to, previous sexual partners.

I knew instantly that this revelation was for me, because though I had broken free in my relationship with Jamie, there were others. I knew I needed to move beyond unhealthy relationships of my past but I wasn't sure where to start. I knew that The Lord had forgiven me, but I wanted my mind to be free from any residual bondage, any thoughts that kept me tied to the past, no matter how crazy it sounded to me.

It wasn't just about the times that I had been in a physical relationship. The emotional abandonment that I never confronted allowed me to form unhealthy attachments to several people, even in my thought life. There were times I had become obsessed with a few individuals that I felt would be perfect for me. Dreaming, wishing and planning my life around what could happen if those individuals would give me a chance. There were moments when these individuals consumed my every waking thought.

This new revelation was another step in the journey, helping me to realize this behavior was part of my codependent nature that needed to be healed.

Emotional ties aren't always physical, although 1 Corinthians 6:16 and Genesis 2:24 clearly help us to understand that physical relationships create a bond: *The two are united as one.* Jesus said:

> ...A man leaves father and mother and is firmly bonded to his wife, becoming one flesh—no longer two bodies but one.
> —Matthew 19:5 MSG

Sexually intimate relationships outside of marriage commitment can be damaging, especially if both people are promiscuous. There's a reason Paul says, "Run from sexual sin! No other sin so clearly affects the body as this one does," 1 Corinthians 6:18.

I like this explanation from Kris Vallotton. In his blog he writes: "Sex is like gluing two pieces of wood together and the next day ripping them apart. Of course, wood from the opposite board remains on each board. A piece of your sex partner (the good, bad, and ugly) stays with you (and vice versa) for the rest of your life. You can only imagine what it looks like when you bond with multiple partners."[2]

As I said before, the soul-tie can happen in other ways, besides sexual intimacy.

TRUTH BE TOLD

Speaking of Christian television, it can be polarizing — for both Christians and non-Christians. I agree with the idiomatic expression, "Don't throw out the baby with the bath water". As in ANYTHING, we must be discerning. Just because something looks ridiculous doesn't mean it can't be used of God. Conversely, just because something looks pious doesn't mean it is right. Let God be God and use what He chooses. We can get so hung up on how things are supposed to look that we miss what God is saying. Have we ever looked the other way or scoffed at something just because it didn't appeal to our nature? Do we ever actually fight against what He is trying to do because what we see in the natural doesn't take into account our supernatural God? In order to see through the natural to His supernatural, He has to change our nature.

Remember Balaam?

"Then the Lord gave the donkey the ability to speak. "What have I done to you that deserves your beating me three times?" it asked Balaam. "You have made me look like a fool!" Balaam shouted. "If I had a sword with me, I would kill you!" "But I am the same donkey you have ridden all your life," the donkey answered. "Have I ever done anything like this before?" "No," Balaam admitted. Then the Lord opened Balaam's eyes, and he saw the angel of the Lord standing in the roadway with a drawn sword in his hand. Balaam bowed his head and fell face down on the ground before him."
—Numbers 22:28-31

Soul-ties can be created with people or things because we begin to idolize them, placing them between us and God, even above God in our eyes. There were times in my past when I wanted a connection so badly, I allowed my thought life concerning others — my imaginations — to monopolize me. On several occasions I desperately acted on those fantasies, trying to make connections with people by sending notes or setting up situations to spend time where I knew they would be. Even people I barely knew.

I started praying as Holy Spirit lead me to pray, naming each person that I had been intimate with, relationships in which I had developed an unhealthy attachment, even those who I idolized in my mind. I prayed, breaking any "soul-tie" — any emotional bond that had been created. Then I began praying for each person. This exercise or exorcise as it were, helped me to let go of any lingering feelings, or attachments — any unhealthy bond that was created.

As I prayed through these relationships, I began to realize that the One who loved me more than I could ever imagine was the only One who mattered. I sought Him more and more. He continued to renew my mind as I continued to draw close to Him.

> But whenever someone turns to the Lord, the veil is taken away. For the Lord is the Spirit, and wherever the Spirit of the Lord is, there is freedom. So all of us who have had that veil removed can see and reflect the glory of the Lord. And the Lord—who is the Spirit—makes us more and more like Him as we are changed into his glorious image. —2 Corinthians 3:16-18

No longer did the fear of abandonment have a death grip on me. Were there moments when the familiar feelings tried to creep back in? Certainly, but most of the time I recognized them right away and was able to fight them with scripture — like Galatians 2:20 and 2 Corinthians 5:17— and in the name of Jesus.

That's another truth I learned from tribe member, Wanda. Wanda had walked through some tough places too. She openly shared the Godly wisdom she gained. One day we were talking about repeated attacks from the enemy in the familiar places of our mind. Her wisdom gave me confidence.

She explained that once we walk through a healing process with the Lord, we become more aware of the enemy's devices. We are more able to quickly recognize when the enemy of our souls tries to take us by surprise. Those areas that were meant to destroy us, the Lord uses for our good. If we continue to lean into Him and His Word, we are armed and ready and the fight is not as hard, because we know the Lord as Deliverer.

LOVE OF ANOTHER KIND – PART 2

BREAKING FREE

For the first time in my life I didn't feel the need to be in a relationship with another person in order to be whole. It was an odd and exhilarating place to be. I had never experienced such freedom. It was something only God could do.

I was finally on the outside of the cage, looking in. There was still healing to do, but never again would I be trapped in that space.

I had a new heart. A new nature. Every step I took, even the missteps, I took with the Lord. Instead of trying to hide, I walked everything out with Him.

> *And I will give you a new heart, and I will put a new spirit in you. I will take out your stony, stubborn heart and give you a tender, responsive heart.*
> *—Ezekiel 36:26*

There were other changes too. I got a new job. My mom moved to a new place so I moved back in with my dad and stepmom, which was another layer of healing and restoration.

It was an amazing time. My relationship with Jesus was enough. It truly was and continues to be a love of another kind.

> *My beloved is mine, and I am his. —Song of Songs 2:16 NIV*

Dear friend: Are you in the struggle, trying to walk out this healing process? Or have you just realized there are some things you need to confront, deal with and release? I simply want to offer this — you can make it. Jesus is for you. No two stories are the same, yet He understands what you're going through. According to John 10:10, His desire is that you be whole and healed, living abundantly with Him. I am praying for you and I offer this prayer right now:

"Father, I pray for the one reading this book right now. You know where they are, You see them and You love them. Hebrews 4:15 says that Jesus, our High Priest understands our weaknesses, for He faced all of the same testings we do... So we come boldly before Your throne of grace and find Your mercy and grace awaiting us there. Please help us in this moment to allow you to begin making changes in our hearts, our minds and our spirits that move us toward You, into a deeper relationship with You. Thank You Holy Spirit for revealing the love of God to us and helping us to understand that Your love is truly the beginning of everything else in our lives. Thank You that You know us, You understand us like no other and You will help us find our way to the freedom Jesus gives us. Amen."

[1] *Change Your Nature*. Writer: Winans, Benjamin. Copyright © 1987 Sparrow Song (BMI) (adm. at CapitolCMGPublishing.com) All rights reserved.

[2] Vallotton, Kris. Kris Vallotton Blog. *7 SIGNS OF AN UNHEALTHY SOUL TIE*, May 03, 2019 https://www.krisvallotton.com/7-signs-of-an-unhealthy-soul-tie

MUSIC NOTES, CH 8: *Change Your Nature*, as recorded by Bebe & Cece Winans (love them!!) was life changing for me. I loved every song on this sophomore release from the siblings, but this one in particular gave me hope that the Lord could do a work deep, deep inside of me. Another song from this album that turned me inside out was *In Return*, written by their brother Marvin Winans. Just listen to them both.

Find *Change Your Nature* on YouTube at: https://youtu.be/0b-N8JOWUCw or in iTunes at: https://music.apple.com/us/album/change-your-nature/724655413?i=724655603

Find *In Return* on YouTube at: https://youtu.be/W7nayPW-ceE or in iTunes at: https://music.apple.com/us/album/in-return/724655413?i=724655654

In Return. Writer: Winans, Marvin L. In Return [Recorded by BeBe & CeCe Winans]. Copyright © 1987 New Spring Publishing Inc. (ASCAP) Selah Publishing (ASCAP) (adm. at CapitolCMGPublishing.com) All rights reserved.

Chapter 9

LOVE IS A WONDERFUL THING
A WONDERFUL, COMPLICATED THING

Love stories are so... subjective. What speaks love to you may not mean anything to me but as human beings, to be loved and known are some of our deepest felt needs. TV and movies are filled fairytale endings. I think deep inside, we all hope for that.

I am keenly aware that what you are about to read isn't the way relationships work out for so many people, but this is my story. Your story may be different. Maybe you're still on this journey. Perhaps God is still writing your story and your ending will be extraordinary. No two stories are the same. They are as different and unique as you or I.

REGARDING DAVID

In the days following my soul-tie-breaking experiment — praying and releasing those agreements and covenants I had made physically, emotionally and spiritually — I kept coming back to praying about David. My heart continued to soften towards him.

I felt I owed my spiritual turn around in part to David. His obedience to the Lord through a simple phone call and an invitation to come to church had been an answer to my secret prayer. Though David didn't know to the full extent, that amazing night the Lord set me on a trajectory that completely turned my life around.

Days turned into weeks and winter turned into spring as I continued to reflect on and pray about David. While I no longer felt the need to be in a relationship to be whole, processing all of these things with the Lord made me realize that I did actually love David. That realization, however, didn't come with any guarantee. Though he had been a huge factor in my recent 180, our dating years had been filled with friction. We had hurt one another so badly. What's more, in my mind, I had strayed so far out of the "Christian norm" when it came to relationships, it was not possible for us to be together.

After college, David planned on going into the ministry. I assumed that he needed a certain type of wife — what I envisioned a pastor's wife should be and I didn't fit the mold. In fact, while he was home for the summer, David dated a beautiful and godly young woman, Victoria. From the outside looking in, they seemed like a perfect match.

I got to observe them a lot that summer, as many of us who ran around as teenagers still traveled in the same friend-group. Though David and I had multiple opportunities to chat, we didn't converse much. We were very cordial, but nothing more.

MOVING FORWARD

So I moved from praying about him to praying for him. As far as any further relationship with David was concerned, I put it all before the Lord. Though part of me wanted to get married and all of the things that most 25-year-old women want, in my heart I was okay if I never married. I had such peace. Being wholly content in my relationship with the Lord for the first time ever was proving to be one of the most precious times in my life.

In the middle of all of this, that same Associate Pastor who dropped those life-verses on me a few months before, shared this verse as he opened up the church service one evening:

> *A man's heart plans his way,*
> *But the Lord directs his steps.*
> *—Proverbs 16:9 NKJV*

Another truth poured into my life at just the right moment.

My tribe continued to offer accountability and help me stay focused on what mattered most. We shared with one another and prayed about a lot of things, including the David situation, but it didn't become an obsession as my thoughts of relationship had in times past.

Yet in the late fall of that year, *I knew* that David was the one for me. It was the first and only time I ever *knew*. It used to drive me crazy when people would talk about being in love. Often I would hear them say, "I just knew so and so was the one..." but I never knew, in any relationship I'd ever been in. Up to this point, all of my serious relationships were attempts at filling the void in my life, including my earlier relationship with David. Yet this time, even though *I knew* I loved him, that didn't mean that I knew he loved me.

Remember, God has a sense of humor and irony that is better than anyone. Ever. This time *I knew* that David was the one. He had no clue.

So my tribe and I prayed and I kept moving forward. I had dates with a few other guys. I didn't date anyone seriously, but I didn't sit at home pining away. I prayed, waited, trusted the Lord and made the most of life.

There was one guy I dated off and on throughout my early 20's. I loved and still love Marshall dearly, but I wasn't in love with him. We grew up together, we always had a blast and we were both very creative souls. I loved his family and they loved me, but I just couldn't allow myself to get really close to him, because *I knew*. I kept telling him that we could only be friends. I'm not sure that he believed me. Given our history, he could have thought that I was playing hard to get, but I wasn't. *I knew*. Even though nothing was happening between David and me, *I knew*.

One evening just around Christmas, I was hanging out at Marshall's house. His brother-in-law, who was a pastor, sat me down in the family's dining room. I'll never forget what he said to me, "Denise, I just feel like the Lord wants me to tell you to hang on. That relationship that you have been praying and waiting for is right around the corner so be patient. We all really hope that this means Marshall, but even if not, the Lord wants you to wait for His timing."

I was blown away. I just sat there and cried. I didn't know what to say, but his words were the confirmation I needed, even though it did not involve Marshall. With a grateful heart I went home that night knowing I had just heard from the Lord. Steadfastly I was willing to wait. Little did I know a few days later everything would change.

THEY THAT WAIT HAVE TO ALSO BE PATIENT

My heart was so excited because I sensed that the Lord was working in ways I could not see. During that holiday season our friend-group got together often. In my excitement I wanted to tell David that *I knew* each time I had the opportunity — but I waited. I heard what the Lord said and I obeyed. I didn't jump ahead. I had done that enough in my life.

The one thing I understood clearly from the Lord was this: when the time came to talk to David, I was to ask him to forgive me. In all this time, we'd never had *that* conversation. There was so much I wanted to say to him. I just wanted to come clean with it all.

A few times when David was in close proximity, I would ask the Lord, "Can I talk to him now?"

He would whisper back, "Not yet."

The night before New Year's Eve, which happened to be a Sunday, our group of friends had a gathering after church. I platonically rode with Marshall. After a few hours of talking, eating and much laughter, the party was wrapping up. I heard David talking about his schedule for the next few days. He was leaving soon because Power Unlimited was doing a recording over the winter break. At that moment I heard Holy Spirit whisper, "Now!" My heart leapt inside my chest. I waited for David to finish talking and then seized the opportunity.

"Hey!" I almost shouted.

"Hey!" He smiled.

"Do you have time to spend some time with me before you go back to school?" I smiled back, heart still pounding.

"Sure!" He replied. "Why don't I pick you up for lunch tomorrow?"

"That sounds great!" I managed, without a squeal. We made plans and everyone said goodnight.

As Marshall drove me home I could barely contain my excitement, but it was more about finally getting to share my heart than anything else. I prayed that night that the Lord's will would be done in all of our lives, including Marshall's. I wasn't sure exactly what I was going to say at lunch the next day — I only knew that it had to begin with forgiveness. The Lord hadn't failed me yet. He would give me the words to say.

New Years Eve Day, David and I opened up years of dialogue over a blueberry bagel with blueberry cream cheese. I asked him to forgive me — for our unhealthy relationship early on, the bad break-ups and my personal failings that caused so much hurt. He was so gracious and to my surprise, he asked me to forgive him too. I wasn't looking for that, but there was a lot of healing going on in those moments. We talked and shared so easily. I really sensed that more restoration was being done than I could understand.

In my mind, I prayed. "Can I tell him I love him?"

Holy Spirit said, "Not yet."

That was good enough for me. David took me home. I felt lighter than air. It was a great day and *I knew* that I would get to see him that night. Our friend and mutual tribe member, Dennis, was hosting a huge New Year's Eve party. Everyone would be there. I was looking forward to it.

A NEW YEAR

I rode to the party with my friend, Hope. We got to the house about 8 pm and opened the door. There was David ... with Victoria. My heart sank a little, but I had to trust what I had heard from the Lord.

Hope and I left for a bit to attend the New Year's Eve service at church. The party was still in full swing when we returned, however, David was gone. I was guessing that Victoria had to be home by a certain time but I quickly learned that wasn't the case. Though she didn't have to be home, David took her home by midnight — then he came back.

He and I talked and flirted and sat by one another all evening. It was almost as if we were testing "us" out, to see if we still fit. About 4 am the few of us that were left decided to go to Denny's® for breakfast. There wasn't enough room for all of us in one vehicle, so I road with Hope.

On the way, Hope decided that she needed to go home after we ate and that I needed to find my own ride home. When we got to the restaurant I asked the group if someone would be willing to give me a ride home after breakfast. David volunteered.

After we ate, the last of us piled into David's car to make the trek back to Dennis' house. I sat in the back seat. David caught my eye a few times while looking in the rear view mirror. I thought my heart would burst. There was a beautiful Blue Moon that night. It was so bright, so full of promise.

When the party was over at nearly 6 am, David drove me to my house, moonlight leading the way. We chatted for few moments.

As we hugged goodbye, I whispered, "I don't want to let go..."

David whispered back, "Then don't."

I began to cry — huge crocodile tears all over his leather jacket. It was a sacred moment. We didn't even notice my dad come outside until we were startled by his truck engine revving up. He was getting ready to go to work.

We didn't kiss. We didn't make any promises, though in my heart, *I knew*. A few days later David asked me if I wanted to meet him for lunch before he headed back to school. Of course I agreed. We talked about a lot of different things, including Victoria. He let me know that things weren't as serious as they looked.

Our college years were coming to a close and we were both praying about the future. I didn't know it at the time, but David says he knew how he felt about me, he just wasn't sure if he was willing to open himself back up to me. So much had transpired and though he knew he loved me, his first priority was to his calling. He needed some clarity from The Lord.

IN THE MEANTIME

Meanwhile, I kept talking to the Lord about everything. Here are few passages from my journal, that same journal that began with a cry for help:

> *Journal Entry: "January 6 … I miss David. I want to see him, to be with him, to talk and know how we are together. And sometimes I begin to take for granted that he's mine again. But he's not. And I have to let You do it…*
>
> *I want to be around him to be sure it's what we both want! But there's no chance right now.*
>
> *No matter what — You are my God — and I will serve You — David or no David, husband or no husband, You have called me….*

My birthday was only a few days after he went back to college. I wasn't sure if he would even remember:

> *Journal Entry: "January 10 … He called! He called! What a great day!?! Thank You, Lord for helping us.*
>
> *All is quiet now. Everything in the house is still, except for my pen.*
>
> *Outside the wind is blowing the barren trees around on this cold day.*
>
> *But to me, it is a beautiful day. Not because it's my birthday. Not because David called.*
>
> *But because on the outside things looked bleak and dreary. The winds were blowing my life around and it looked like the sun may never shine again.*
>
> *And You, my Savior, looked inside me to the stillness of my heart and in a single moment gave me hope that soon the sun would shine again.*
>
> *…even on those days when it had to rain, or snow or just blow around, You were there inside of me, so that I could see everything around me in a new way.*

I sent David a card for his birthday a few weeks later. I took a Holy Spirit step of faith, making sure I heard His voice with the card I chose. The inside sentiment read: "A love like ours comes along once in a Blue Moon." It seemed perfect and there was no taking it back once I dropped it in the mailbox. Years later I learned that David's heart began to fully open up to me after reading that card. The Lord is in the details.

STRANGE THINGS AFOOT

Unbeknownst to me, two things were happening about that time. One, David's parents were against our dating again. Who could blame them? They watched me fall from grace and claw my way back. They had nothing against me as a person. They just didn't want their son to be in a serious relationship with me. And two, David was planning a surprise trip home to see me for Valentine's Day.

Dennis and several friends found a way to get me out of the house and to the church that night. We were planning activities for an upcoming meeting — I just didn't know the preparations were going to take hours. They kept stalling me to keep me at church but I really wanted to be home because I just *knew* he was going to call. (Back then, one had to be home to receive a phone call.) I used the phone in the church lobby several times to call the house checking to see if David called. My heart dropped a little each time. The answer with every ring was, "No."

It was getting late, nearly 11 pm and I was getting in my car to leave when my friends told me I had to stay. Their reasoning wasn't making any sense when suddenly I saw headlights pulling into the church parking lot. It was David! My friends were overjoyed that they were able to keep me until he arrived — having driven through a blizzard to make it home for Valentine's Day. It was so romantic. We went to Frisch's at midnight and had pumpkin pie and hot chocolate.

A few weeks later several of us took a friend-trip to see David and our friend (and his roommate, Eddie). Eddie dated my good friend Shelly, so we traveled together having many prayer meetings driving down the road. (We watched and prayed.) On that trip, David and I told one another, "I love you."

From that moment before we realized it, we were on the road to marriage.

In our church world, promiscuous lifestyles that I came out of were frowned upon. David was called to serve the Lord through music ministry.

> **MY SHARONA**
>
> Our "Tribe" was all in with us, even in the everyday moments.
>
> Sharon, who has been a part of all of my triumphs, many adventures and is still one of my very best friends, has always spoken the truth in love.
>
> One Sunday while David was home for a visit we were all sitting together in church. David and I were holding hands and I was so happy that he was there, I kept rubbing his arm as if at any second he could go away.
>
> It was surely driving her crazy because Sharon turned to me and whispered sharply in love as only she can do, "If you don't stop it, you're going to rub his skin off."
>
> We all had a good laugh, but I knew she was keeping me grounded. I will love her forever for that and so much more.

Because of what I'd been through, he met with our Pastor to see if he should pursue the relationship with me all the way to marriage. If our relationship would hinder that call in any way, though he loved me fiercely, he was willing to take a step back.

Pastor Timmerman told him assuredly, "David, if there is a church out there that won't accept Denise, then they are in the wrong business."

David could see that indeed, the Lord had changed my nature. I'm not saying that David is perfect, although I used to tell him that! Yet when I look back over my life, I see how the Lord has used him over and over again to love me as Christ loves the church, His bride (Ephesians 5:25).

David wasn't my savior, but he pointed me to Jesus.

Upon reflection, we realized we both had so much to learn and so many places inside of us that needed healing before we made a commitment to one another. The Lord has given us a beautiful love story, filled with forgiveness, grace, miracles and the hand of God everywhere. Our tribe stood by our sides and lined the aisle at our wedding.

DREAMS & CALLINGS

Often I reflect with a smile on God's sense of humor — the irony of David telling me I was the one to my *knowing* he was the one. As a married couple, we've had our share of bumps along the way and we were and are far from perfect.

David continues to show Christlike love in so many ways. Time and time he has again reinforced God's calling on my life. It wasn't just *he* who was called. It is *we* who have been called.

My dreams of leading worship and leading others to Jesus have been realized throughout our entire marriage. I get to lead worship every weekend, with my husband. I've had opportunities to lead worship at women's conferences, my husband and his band with us all the way. I've directed choirs. I've taught at conferences, in Sunday school, directed and acted in musicals, led Bible Studies and more.

David has never discouraged me in my pursuit of ministry or business. Never once has he said, "Perhaps you shouldn't do that, given your past." Never once.

Quite the opposite is true. He has encouraged me to pursue the calling of God at every step. David recognized creative abilities in me that even I didn't know I had and encouraged me to pursue them with abandon. If I have ever needed anything to help me succeed, he has done his best to make sure my need was supplied.

Isn't that what Jesus does for us, as individuals who comprise *The Church*? He promises that He will be with us all the way, "even until the end of the age," Matthew 28:20b. His word encourages us to "stir up the gift" we have been given — to find ways to use those creative gifts He has placed inside of us, "… This is why I remind you to fan into flames the spiritual gift God gave you when I laid my hands on you," 2 Timothy 1:6. Paul tells us that Lord will give us everything we need to accomplish His work "according to His glorious riches," Philippians 4:19.

#grateful

Grateful doesn't begin to describe my thoughts and feelings toward my husband. Life gets crazy sometimes. We get busy doing what we do and sometimes we begin to lose sight of each other. The Lord only has to remind me of this beautiful gift He's given me in my husband. We're not perfect. We've let one another down and helped pick one another back up. David has been my best friend for over 30 years now. He still makes my heart pound. We have this beautiful family in Devin, Ashley & Samuel and we have been blessed to live near our extended families for the past 15 years. We are truly blessed.

The Lord continues to fulfill the dreams He placed in me, even from over 30 years ago. Recently, our church services had to be live-streamed — along with most of the rest of the country. One morning my prayer partners met with me before church. As we were praying, seemingly out of the blue, the Lord brought something to my mind.

"Live-streaming goes everywhere. Across the country. Across the world. Even to Romania."

Jesus' ways never go against His word, even if our some of our life choices get in the way. Even if situations don't play out the way we thought they would. Sometimes we get in the way, but even then, if we will redirect and submit to His ways, He will carry out a plan for our lives that will blow our minds. It's so much better His way.

> *For God's gifts and his call can never be withdrawn. —Romans 11:29*

There is so much to tell about our sweet love story. I could fill another book with the ways The Lord has woven our lives together. I might do that someday. The reason I write about David in this book is this: He has been the epitome of Christlike love in my life. He has been an example to me of my Kinsmen Redeemer[1], who reached out through all of the wreck that was my life, my pain, abandonment and rejection to show me the love of Jesus.

This is what the heart of this book is about. How we, the Bride of Christ, can be *The Church*, we can be Jesus' hands and feet, we can show and give and live out — His love — in *every* relationship we have.

UNLIKELY GRACE

And I am certain that God, who began the good work within you, will continue his work until it is finally finished on the day when Christ Jesus returns. —Philippians 1:6

I wrote a song for our wedding day. Debbie helped me chart it out and get it ready to sing to David. Johnna helped organize the whole wedding and gave me my wedding day joke — a tradition in her family to give the bride something to think about and laugh at during wedding day jitters. Our tribe surrounded us and stood with us that beautiful day.

Looking back at our wedding pictures, there were tears all around, including my dad, who was trying to hold it together as he walked me down the aisle. Our tribe, including the guys, were wiping their eyes. Even as I sang to David I could barely make it through the song without weeping at the goodness of God.

Pastor Timmerman remarked that in order to keep himself from crying, he kept trying to make eye contact with someone in church who wasn't crying — but he was unable.

So many were rejoicing with us on that day. My song, though simple, speaks to God's faithfulness in our lives.

*"His promises are true, He has a love that's kind and faithful,
He's blessed my life with you, He's proved to us He's more than able,
To take us through the storms of life, and help each other through,
Now we're becoming man and wife, for His promises are true."[2]*

---

[1]*Kinsman Redeemer is a male relative who, according to various laws found in the Pentateuch, had the privilege or responsibility to act for a relative who was in trouble, danger, or need of vindication. This is what Jesus Christ did for all of humanity. Although David is not my relative, his actions toward me epitomized Christ's sacrificial love. https://www.biblestudytools.com/dictionary/kinsman-redeemer/*

[2]*Songwriter: Chaney, Denise. ©1991 His Promises Are True.*

MUSIC NOTES, CH 9: I was listening a lot to Amy Grant (which I very often did). One song that really spoke to me while I was praying for David was *If These Walls Could Speak* written by Jimmy Webb. I can't put the lyric here, but as I said in the beginning of the chapter, I began to feel that I owed my spiritual turn around in part to David. If you listen, pay attention to the last several stanzas. Sometimes a whole song will leap out at you, sometimes certain phrases. This was the case with this song.

As for Amy, my love for her and her music goes back many, many years.

Find *If These Walls Could Speak* on YouTube at: https://youtu.be/5FPkVvtm5TA or in iTunes at: https://music.apple.com/us/album/if-these-walls-could-speak/1442917329?i=1442917949

If These Walls Could Speak. Songwriter: Webb, Jimmy. [As recorded by Amy Grant on Lead Me On]. © 1988 (adm. at Universal Music Publishing Group) All rights reserved.

PART 2

So here's what I want you to do, God helping you: Take your everyday, ordinary life—your sleeping, eating, going-to-work, and walking-around life—and place it before God as an offering. Embracing what God does for you is the best thing you can do for him. Don't become so well-adjusted to your culture that you fit into it without even thinking. Instead, fix your attention on God. You'll be changed from the inside out. Readily recognize what he wants from you, and quickly respond to it. Unlike the culture around you, always dragging you down to its level of immaturity, God brings the best out of you, develops well-formed maturity in you.
—Romans 12:1-2 MSG

Chapter 10

A NEW MIND

PRESENT DAY

One morning while I was spending time with The Lord, my mind began to drift to a faraway place. I started to follow.

We have choices, you know? Out of nowhere thoughts can pop into our mind that derail our attention or captivate our imagination. Sometimes it's like our thoughts are stuck in a loop — a thought pattern we can't seem to escape. The location my mind was trying to take me had become a well worn path for me. My own solutions to some difficult situations frequently seemed to end the same speculative way.

Among other things, my business hadn't been doing well. Financially as a family we had been going backwards. I had creative ideas that I just *knew* would bring income yet they seemed to lead nowhere. I began imagining ways to get out from under the pressure I was experiencing, like winning the lottery — of course you have to play to win — and other crazy notions, including remembering ways He had met needs in the past and trying to think of how to live that out — again.

The Lord has given many of us great imaginations and creativity. I was allowing mine to flow freely, but not in alignment with Him. He calls us to use these gifts, like imagination and creativity, but to do so out of the overflow of our relationship with Him. His Word. His Spirit.

He had been dealing with me about these thoughts of mine. I was so busy living life that I didn't realize how my thoughts continuously tried to take me to a destination that was far away from Him. His purposes. His plans.

Knowing that I needed to get these unbridled thoughts under control for good, I began to pray for what seemed like the thousandth time: "Lord, I cast down every vain imagination, every thought, every solution that is contrary to You, Your Word, Your Ways!"

> *We are human, but we don't wage war as humans do. We use God's mighty weapons, not worldly weapons, to knock down the strongholds of human reasoning and to destroy false arguments. We destroy every proud obstacle that keeps people from knowing God. We capture their rebellious thoughts and teach them to obey Christ.*
> *—2 Corinthians 10:3-5*

All at once a familiar, scriptural concept came to mind. I prayed aloud, "Create a new thought pattern in me, Lord!" Instantly my mind went to Isaiah:

> *But forget all that— it is nothing compared to what I am going to do. For I am about to do something new. See, I have already begun! Do you not see it? I will make a pathway through the wilderness. I will create rivers in the dry wasteland. —Isaiah 43:18-19*

Literally in my mind's eye I could see tiny streams of water creating new pathways in those desolate places. Slowly I began to release those thoughts that lead to nowhere. Instead, I began to listen to Him regarding my finances and the situations surrounding my business.

REMEMBER... NOT?

This whole exchange between He and I that morning reminded me why I started writing this book in the first place. My heart caught in my chest and began to pound as I recalled my love for *The Church*, my love for the lost, the hurting, the broken and my understanding of what the love of Jesus can do through a people who love Him and have His heart.

I believe that what the Lord was reinforcing in me that day is that: 1) He is God and I am not and 2) as God, what He is doing in my life and on the earth most likely will not look like what I think or imagine it should. Travel along with me as I explore this stream.

The children of Israel had issues with the familiar too. If we begin reading Isaiah 43 at verse 15 (please read the whole chapter) God reminds Israel who He is and what He's done and then He says this seemingly confusing statement: "But forget about all that...."

"Forget about what I did yesterday. Don't dwell in the past. Don't count on Me doing it the same way twice. Don't limit yourself to your own imagination. Look for Me in fresh and new ways."

If you think about it, how God delivered the children of Israel out of Egypt was all done in mind-blowing, new ways:

- God sent a deliverer — Moses;
- Who himself, heard from a talking, flaming-but-never-burning-up bush what his next moves should be;
- Which, among other things, like confronting Pharaoh, was to paint the blood of lambs over the doorposts in order to be saved from the plagues God was sending;
- That act allowed the Israelites to walk out of Egypt with more than they ever had;
- And when their proverbial backs were against a wall (of water), God made the Red Sea stand up for them to cross over on dry ground!
- All NEW THINGS which no one had ever seen.

Yet in Isaiah, God recounted all of that history and then told them "...forget all of that!" In other words, "Don't count or rely on any of that — what I did yesterday — rely on Me. I've got more in store for you!"

What He'd done was amazing! But they needed amazing help again. How could they simply forget these amazing, miraculous feats? Yet He had more waiting for them. More waiting for us than we could ever imagine (ask or think, Ephesians 3:20) because He is Creator God who has an infinite number of ways to care for His children.

He had more ways than I knew how to ask, imagine or think that morning I was when I was endeavoring to imagine all my issues away.

STREAMS IN THE DESERT

What if? What if the children of Israel didn't do any of the things Moses told them to do in order to be freed... because it was unheard of? Or because it had never been done that way before?

Do I do that? Do you?

Think about it. No one expects to see a stream in the desert. It's unheard of. We're not talking about a puddle or pool of water in the sand. We're talking stream. A stream attracts life — whether it's in the desert or elsewhere. A stream of living water is vital. And a stream in the desert? Life-sustaining!

Do we shy away from the adventure God has in store for us because it doesn't make sense to our finite minds? He hasn't changed. He's still the same, but there is so much about our God that we don't yet know. Quite often His ways are new to us because we are still learning all that He is. He gives us these streams in our wastelands to sustain us, to give us life, to teach us more about who He is... so that we, in turn, can bring others to this Living Water.

Peter, in Matthew 16:15-16, had just gotten through having this spirit-filled revelation of who Jesus was. "'Then he asked them, 'But who do you say I am?' Simon Peter answered, 'You are the Messiah, the Son of the living God.'"

My imagination sees that moment almost like an out-of-body experience for Peter. One of those amazing moments when the brain, the mouth and the very core of our being is in alignment with Holy Spirit. To have Jesus tell you that what you just said was a revelation that could only come from the Father — think about that! And upon *that* Revelation *The Entire Church* would be built. What a rush that must have been?!

Yet as we read on, not 30-seconds (or four verses later) in our Bible (there could have been a lapse in actual time) Jesus is telling Peter that he is being used of Satan. Matthew 16:23, "Jesus turned to Peter and said, 'Get away from me, Satan! You are a dangerous trap to me. You are seeing things merely from a human point of view, not from God's.'"

...seeing things merely from a human point of view, not from God's...

Therein lies the issue for us. Do we look at our situation, our circumstance dare I say it — even other people — from our viewpoint? Our perspective? Peter had this spectacular moment with Jesus where everything he spoke and understood in that moment was true, yet he didn't see the bigger picture Jesus was painting.

Jesus knew that in order for *The Church* to be built on this Rock, The Messiah had to die. It was so contrary to everything the Jews had imagined their Messiah would be. He was going to free them from oppression and set up His kingdom ... but dying was His plan all along even though to them it was a new ... thing... and it was the only way for the church to become *The Church*.

I LOVE THE CHURCH

I do love *The Church*. Over half my life now has been serving *The Church* alongside my husband. *The Church* is a powerful moving force. I'm not talking about a power in the way we worship — intense worship services where people cry, shout or run, though I have experienced and enjoyed those moments. I'm not talking about a service we attend once a week that follows an outline, formula or ritual. I'm not even talking about a church meeting, though *The Church* should meet together.

I'm talking about a people who love Him so much that we put aside our own prejudices, desires, even sometimes or own comfort to love like He loves. A *Church*, a people, who understand that God LOVES everyone. EVERYONE.

> *For this is how God loved the world: He gave his one and only Son, so that everyone who believes in him will not perish but have eternal life. God sent his Son into the world not to judge the world, but to save the world through him. —John 3:16-17*

I want to be a person who embodies "but for the grace of God, there go I".[1] I want to live with passion, remembering that God's grace made the difference in my life. I want to live with purpose in order to fulfill God's destiny, not only for my life, but for the lives of those with whom I intersect — in order to share His heart and my story.

> *Instead, you must worship Christ as Lord of your life. And if someone asks about your hope as a believer, always be ready to explain it. But do this in a gentle and respectful way. Keep your conscience clear. Then if people speak against you, they will be ashamed when they see what a good life you live because you belong to Christ. Remember, it is better to suffer for doing good, if that is what God wants, than to suffer for doing wrong!*
> *—1 Peter 3:15-17*

I want to be a part of a people who understand that this life is not all about "me". Instead, I want to be obedient, even when I don't see the whole picture.

The point is not how **much** we *do* or *give*. It's about staying connected to the Father so that when He presents us with opportunities, we can realize it is Him and even if it doesn't look like anything we've done before, we can follow through. Whether that is being salt and light, or His hands and feet, or a city on a hill, we can give hope and share the goodness of God.

> *But you are not like that, for you are a chosen people. You are royal priests, a holy nation, God's very own possession. As a result, you can show others the goodness of God, for he called you out of the darkness into his wonderful light. —1 Peter 2:9*

Because of being in church for most of my life, I have heard these scriptures. Maybe 100's of times throughout my life. I have read these truths, that once made my heart pound with the excitement of winning the world for Jesus. Maybe you can relate. The problem I find is if I'm not staying connected to Him, my own perspective starts to take over. My thoughts become narrowed, diminished, even limited by my worldview into a way of thinking that doesn't line up with the Word.

The thought patterns that I had to cast down that morning had to do with my own way of working out a problem. My own solution. My own level of comfort. I had to break out of those old ways of thinking in order to see His will. His way. It's so much better His way.

There's a reason Romans 12:2 reminds us, "Don't copy the behavior and customs of this world, but let God transform you into a new person by changing the way you think. Then you will learn to know God's will for you, which is good and pleasing and perfect." He wasn't saying that to unbelievers. He was saying it to Jesus followers. Verse one of that chapter starts out by saying, "And so dear brothers and sisters…"

Is it possible for us to go to church, work in church even serve at church and still be caught up in "worldly" thinking, human reasoning, Christian stereotyping, and a let's-keep-it-to-ourselves mentality?

Perhaps, but that is not His way.

Holy Spirit wants to renew, reeducate and redirect our thought patterns because,

> *… Those who live according to the flesh set their minds on the things of the flesh, but those who live according to the Spirit, the things of the Spirit. Romans 8:5 NKJV.*

A HARD LOOK INWARD

My life is a testimony of what *The Church* being the *The Church* can look like and I have shared some of that with you, but my heart breaks when I see how we fall short because I know how powerful *The Church* can be. If you've read this far, you understand that I indeed experienced what the love of Jesus can do through a people who love Him and have His heart.

This book is a challenge to you and to me — to us, *The Church*. Can we allow Holy Spirit to cut through our mindsets? Our set-in ways? Our customs? Our traditions? Our prejudices? Even our previous experiences of His greatness? Are we willing to allow Him to give us a renewed mind in order that we can reach a generation and lead them to Jesus? Are we willing to see the streams? Are we willing to let the Word of God infiltrate us?

> *For the word of God is alive and powerful. It is sharper than the sharpest two-edged sword, cutting between soul and spirit, between joint and marrow. It exposes our innermost thoughts and desires.* —Hebrews 4:12

We may not see Him move like He moved yesterday. Being *The Church* is not going to feel like the good, old times. The truth is, most people don't see any relevance in attending church as it stands now. The enemy has created an us vs. them mentality towards *The Church* that even some of us have fallen for.

We, *The Church* are called to be *The Church* in the marketplace, on the streets, at the PTA, on social media, in our homes, at the well, at the homes of Pharisees — even in persecution. Isn't that what Jesus did?

I've had to take a hard look inward many times. Many years ago when we lived and worked at a church in Cleveland, TN, I ran to the local Walmart for groceries. As I was hurrying towards my car there was a group of college students standing outside the doors. A young woman approached me. I recognized her as she sang in one of the music groups at the college. As I was quickly trying to pass by she asked: "Do you know Jesus?"

What rose up in me was not holy — in fact, it was quite the opposite, more like self righteousness. I replied to her, with a smug smile, "Yes, I know Jesus. I go to church here in town. My husband is the worship pastor at ...."

Then she repeated the question: "But do you know Jesus?"

I was incensed... but why? Why did that bother me so? Why couldn't I simply say, "Yes. He's my best friend."

She understood that just because someone goes to church, serves in a church or even works in a church doesn't mean they know Jesus. I took offense at her sincere question because my heart was in a pride-filled place.

Yes, I've had to take a look inward many times.

For the remainder of this writing, will you take a hard look inward with me? Even though my life was forever changed by those who were *The Church*, there were and are moments where I begin to fall back into old thought patterns. Moments that I have to stop and ask The Lord, "Create a new thought pattern in me. I don't want to settle for what I think is best. Even if it means letting go of the old, well worn, well-rehearsed ways."

Remember this Word from Jesus.

> Then Jesus gave them this illustration: "No one tears a piece of cloth from a new garment and uses it to patch an old garment. For then the new garment would be ruined, and the new patch wouldn't even match the old garment. And no one puts new wine into old wineskins. For the new wine

would burst the wineskins, spilling the wine and ruining the skins. New wine must be stored in new wineskins. But no one who drinks the old wine seems to want the new wine. 'The old is just fine,' they say." —Luke 5:36-39

I don't want the old. Even if it is easier. Or more comfortable. Or safer. I want the fresh streams, new wine and the capacity to hold that new wine that only He can give. It may take some stretching, but I want it His way.

There are many lives that need to be saved. Many that need to know the hope of Jesus. Hurting, broken, enslaved, addicted — people — who need us to be the hands and feet of the One who changed our lives, forever. That means staying in tune with Him. His Word. His Spirit. His purposes. His plans. Loving what He loves. Loving *who* He loves.

---

[1]*https://en.wiktionary.org/wiki/there_but_for_the_grace_of_God_go_I#:~:text=A%20paraphrase%20from%20the%20Bible,I%20am...%22.*

MUSIC NOTES, CH 10: *New Wine.* Boom. It's the Word. I make it my prayer. Thank you, Brooke.

Find *New Wine* on https://youtu.be/1ozGKlOzEVc or in iTunes at: https://music.apple.com/us/album/new-wine/1409145285?i=1409145303

Songwriter: Ligertwood, Brooke. New Wine. © 2017 Hillsong Music Publishing

Chapter 11

ABOUT THE BIRDS

PART 2

I was sharing my revelation *About the Birds* with my BFC (best-friend-cousin) one morning over coffee. She offered another perspective on what it could mean to be in the bird cage in the context of *The Church*. She has been a great encourager and companion on this book writing journey. Also, she knows who Buffy and Jody are... just sayin'.

Through our conversation I began to see clearly another type of cage. We are not alone in this cage, rather, we are surrounded by other birds — birds just like us. Could it be that we *The Church* could actually find ourselves comfortably caged-in, in church?

While researching bird walking (remember the TV show Family Affair), I learned that bird owners group like birds together, so that they will learn only the song that they are being trained to learn. It is a point of pride for bird owners. The different kinds of birds are purposefully kept apart in order to not influence one another.[1]

Stop for a moment think about this. When we think about this separation in relation to *The Church*, it's disturbing on so many levels. When we look closely into our communities, are churches operating together? Or are they caught behind denominational lines, racial barriers and just plain divisiveness. Division and divisiveness has never been God's plan.

> *Behold, how good and how pleasant it is for brethren to dwell together in unity!* —Psalm 133:1 NKJV

BEYOND THE WALLS

I have a friend who works hard to motivate The Body of Christ to exercise — to move beyond four walls and into the community. Quite frequently she engages *The Church* to become a part of serving her community's homeless, jobless, hungry, disenfranchised people. A few years ago this friend had a spirit-inspired idea to create a network of churches that would serve as a referral system. Each church would have the opportunity to take part in being Jesus hands and feet but no single church would shoulder the entire load. It was an amazing vision of being *The Church* at large.

The network became functional and existed for several years, yet it never really took off the way my friend envisioned.

Not because the churches didn't want to help those in need.

The problem was that some of the churches in her community wanted to be the only church to meet the need. Some of the churches were trying to find an angle to make sure that those being served would eventually become tithe paying members of their church. Some churches simply didn't want to work with one another.

My heart grieves that this is even a possibility yet I know it is more than possible. I'm calling this separation that exists between churches as dwelling in separate "cages". In business it's called "silos" or the silo mentality.

The Cambridge Dictionary online defines this use of the word silo as: "a part of a company, organization, or system that does not communicate with, understand, or work well with other parts."[2]

"...A silo describes any management system that is unable to operate with any other system, meaning it's closed off from other systems. Silos create an environment of individual and disparate systems within an organization." [3]

We could easily exchange the words "company, organization or system" with *The Church*. If we take an aerial at look *The Church* in general there are visible silos. My brothers and sisters, this ought not to be so.

Our churches don't all have to do the same things the same way — in fact the following passage expresses this truth. We can be big or small, exuberant or conservative, rural or urban, liturgical or even charismatic — but we are called to operate in unity, not in silos or cages. Each church, I believe, has a gift, a uniqueness that appeals to different people in their communities. Just as each person is uniquely called to reach others in their sphere of influence. Our uniqueness however, shouldn't be what separates. Our uniqueness should compliment one another as we operate together.

The Message translation says it like this:

> *You were all called to travel on the same road and in the same direction, so stay together, both outwardly and inwardly. You have one Master, one faith, one baptism, one God and Father of all, who rules over all, works through all, and is present in all. Everything you are and think and do is permeated with Oneness. But that doesn't mean you should all look and speak and act the same. Out of the generosity of Christ, each of us is given his own gift... He handed out gifts of apostle, prophet, evangelist, and pastor-teacher to train Christ's followers in skilled servant work, working within Christ's body, the church...* —Ephesians 4:4-7, 11-12 MSG

THE RICHNESS OF CHRIST'S BODY

As I said before, I have had an interesting relationship with *The Church*. Part of my church experience has been observing the richness of The Body of Christ in operation through other denominations and walks of faith. Thank God for this blessing! I've encapsulated a tiny bit of those experiences here.

The Church of God, Cleveland, TN: This is the movement that God used to establish a spiritual foundation in me. The COG has been my primary church family for almost my entire life. The majority of the experiences I've shared from my earlier days happened within the COG. It was there that I learned about and experienced freedom of worship. I grew to know a God who personally interacts directly and individually with His people. I came to understand my pentecostal heritage as more than shouting and speaking in tongues, but a fire inside that wants to turn the world upside down for Jesus. This group of believers invested so much into a broken little girl. I'm so thankful for my heritage.

The Baptist Years: During my early wandering years I attended a Baptist church full of wonderful, Bible-believing and Bible teaching people. The preaching and the classes I attended contained sound, fundamental biblical teaching. Though the actual church services were more cerebral and not necessarily as demonstrative as I was used to, they were full of the Word. I learned that emotional or not, God was present. He was moving in that place.

The Non-Denominational Beginnings: Shortly after David and I were married, we worked at a large, non-denominational church in a very metropolitan area. It was a culture shock in almost every way, including the transition from the southern Bible belt lifestyle we'd grown accustomed to versus the urban sprawl of the northern Virginia/D.C. area. Yet this church was full of wonderful, diverse people who loved the Lord and I loved doing life with them. We were blessed to get to work there. The Lord began opening our eyes and hearts to the fact that real Christians existed outside of our familiar denominational bubble.

The Free Methodist Church: A bit later, when we took a position at a church in Indianapolis, I was looking for a job. A friend at our new church mentioned that her employer was hiring. Having never heard of the Free Methodist Church (FMC), I didn't realize their World Headquarters was right down the road from us. I'll never forget my job interview there as it was yet another look into a church world unlike my own.

Towards the end of the interview, the Director of the department said something like this: "You come from a denomination where you embrace the gift of glossolalia. Do you feel that you would need to convert or proselytize other employees in the building to your faith tradition?"

First of all, heart-pounding, I was glad that I knew what the terms 'glossolalia' and 'proselytize' meant! And second, in that instant, Holy Spirit brought a scripture to mind that I have endeavored to live by from that moment on.

I answered, "I believe that it is up to each one of us to work out or own salvation with fear and trembling," (Philippians 2:12). I got the job.

Working in that building for five years, I made life-long connections with people who love Jesus and who poured into me. They brought so much to The Kingdom. They were Bible believing and they provided faith-filled publications to the world. The FMC as a whole are missions minded, innovative in higher education and cutting edge with evangelism — just to name a few of the many ways they advance the Kingdom. We had prayer, Bible studies and chapel — at work! I loved it so much.

It was in one of those Bible studies where I learned a fundamental truth. We were studying *Experiencing God* from Baptist leader, Henry Blackaby and his son, Dr. Richard Blackaby. I am paraphrasing, but the principle is this: *God is moving. If we listen to Him, we get to be in on what He is doing.*[4] That truth alone was life altering for me and you will read it repeatedly in this book.

Just because some of the people at the FMC didn't speak in tongues (I say some, because I actually knew those who did) didn't mean that they missed hearing Holy Spirit. Their lives proved that they heard Him and moved with Him, loud and clear.

Berean Christian Stores (Not a "church" per se, but I learned so much about *The Church* there, that I have to include it): A move or so later I went to work for a Christian store chain, actually my most favorite position — so far. I was surrounded by people from almost every faith tradition, yet we worked together with one purpose — to make Bibles, books and resources available for anyone and everyone.

ABOUT THE BIRDS — PART 2

It was there that I was met with some real questions about my faith. Could there possibly be other faith traditions where people loved Jesus as much as I did? Or more? Could there be something to the sacred practices of some churches? Or one of the big question for us Pentecostals — could people casually drink (insert your questionable vice here) and still be Christians? These sincere inquiries represent only a few of many earnest conversations I had with The Lord during that season.

> *Always be humble and gentle. Be patient with each other, making allowance for each other's faults because of your love. Make every effort to keep yourselves united in the Spirit, binding yourselves together with peace. For there is one body and one Spirit, just as you have been called to one glorious hope for the future. There is one Lord, one faith, one baptism, one God and Father of all, who is over all, in all, and living through all.*
> —Ephesians 4:2-6

I'm not going to take it upon myself to answer any of the above questions for you, dear reader, or anyone else. I am simply asking you the same questions that put me on a search to understand His heart for us, *The Church*. I had to study the scripture, asking Holy Spirit to reveal truth — His truth. Not looking through my "this is the way we grew up" lens. Instead, asking Him to help me love, love, love love, not judge. Unity for a common purpose, His purpose, which is to reveal His love, His nature, His truth, His grace — Him — to the world.

I will say this: In all of my experience of working with other Christians, I learned that I had wrongly judged some people on some things that didn't really matter.

WHY?

So why do we, *The Church*, do it? Why do we waste our time criticizing other churches? Why do we separate, isolate, silo or cage ourselves in when together, we can accomplish so much more? Not only that, but in doing so we miss the very instruction the Lord gives us in His Word.

How can we win people for the Kingdom when *The Church* at large doesn't always work together?

There is a Way.

> *... Until we're all moving rhythmically and easily with each other, efficient and graceful in response to God's Son, fully mature adults, fully developed within and without, fully alive like Christ. No prolonged infancies among*

us, please. We'll not tolerate babes in the woods, small children who are an easy mark for impostors. God wants us to grow up, to know the whole truth and tell it in love—like Christ in everything. We take our lead from Christ, who is the source of everything we do. He keeps us in step with each other. His very breath and blood flow through us, nourishing us so that we will grow up healthy in God, robust in love. —Ephesians 4:13-16 MSG

Jesus is our Way. He is our Leader in coming together in unity. No more cages. No more silos. No more separation.

Can we *The Church* move together to impact our cities? Our nation? Our world?

I believe we can. It is happening even now, beginning with you and me.

[1] https://www.npr.org/templates/story/story.php?storyId=102458087

[2] Silo. https://dictionary.cambridge.org/us/dictionary/english/silo

[3] Author, Abby Dykes. Silo Definition & Meaning.. https://www.webopedia.com/definitions/information-silo/

[4] Experiencing God, Henry Blackaby, Richard Blackaby "Watch to see where God is working and join Him in His work."

Note: It was at the FMC where I learned that the Church of God that I knew wasn't the ONLY Church of God ... when I told people that my husband worked for the Church of God, they would ask "Anderson?" I would reply, "Cleveland." It got to be quite comical!

MUSIC NOTES, CH 11: *Ordinary People.* Wow. A trip on the way-back machine for sure, but the lyrics of this song are timeless and true. The Lord wants to use us. We are so blessed to get to partner with Him.

Find *Ordinary People* on YouTube here: https://youtu.be/FOZ8LmYVcVA or in iTunes at: https://music.apple.com/us/album/ordinary-people/724574830?i=724575039

Ordinary People. Songwriter: Hall, Danniebelle. [As recorded by Danniebelle on Remembering the Times]. © 1977 (adm. at Universal Music Publishing Group) All rights reserved.

Chapter 12

A LIGHT IN THE LIGHT

WAIT. WHAT??

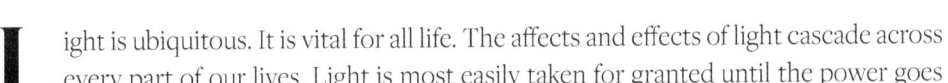

Light is ubiquitous. It is vital for all life. The affects and effects of light cascade across every part of our lives. Light is most easily taken for granted until the power goes out and we are surrounded by darkness.

As Christians, we know and understand that Jesus is the Light. So much of scripture teaches us about light. I love how the first chapter of John weaves us back to the beginning, illuminating Jesus as The Light.

> *In the beginning the Word already existed.*
> *The Word was with God,*
> *and the Word was God.*
> *He existed in the beginning with God.*
> *God created everything through him,*
> *and nothing was created except through him.*
> *The Word gave life to everything that was created,*
> *and his life brought light to everyone.*
> *The light shines in the darkness,*
> *and the darkness can never extinguish it.*
> *—John 1:1-45*

Light. He created it. He gave it. We have it. This life-giving light. It's vital to our being... and easily kept to ourselves. I think that's why the Word gives us so many reminders and illustrations about light — Matthew 5:14, 1 John 1:7, Ephesians 5:8, 1 Peter 2:9 — just a few of the over 260 references to light, depending on which version you study.

The use of the word light in the above references is the word phōs (5457 in Strong's Concordance[1]) meaning: light, a source of light, radiance. A little more explanation from HELPS™[2] Word-Studies: phōs (a neuter noun) – properly, light (especially in terms of its results, what it manifests); in the NT, **the manifestation of God's self-existent life; divine illumination to reveal and impart life, through Christ**.

The Light in us is meant to reveal Jesus to the world.

LIGHT BREAKS THROUGH DARKNESS

A former youth pastor once used the entire congregation in his sermon illustration about Jesus being the Light of the world. All of the windows in the church were already darkened. When he asked for all of the overhead lights to be turned off complete darkness overtook the room.

He then asked one person to turn on the light on their phone. The darkness was instantly repelled by that one light. One light, one small, $300 flashlight, as my husband calls our cell phones, made a difference in that dark room. Imagine, how light permeated the room when the entire congregation participated. You may have seen or been involved in an illustration similar to this one. Incredibly effective, we experienced the impact of one small light.

However, try asking people to shine their phone light with the overhead lights still on. It makes very little difference in illuminating the space. The phone's light can't be seen at all until it's pointed directly in someone's face. The light in the light is barely noticeable. Until it's focused on something specific, it doesn't illuminate anything — it only draws attention to the holder of the phone.

What about us? As church people, do we only allow our Jesus light to be seen in church or around church people and still expect our light to be effective? Often we seem to protect our light...but from what?

> *Jesus spoke to the people once more and said, "I am the light of the world."*
> *—John 8:12a*

Have you ever noticed, when you're trying to sleep, one little light can turn your world upside down? I'll stop at nothing to cover up a light that is disturbing my sleep. I've used socks to cover up the light of a cable box or an alarm clock. I've even used an eye mask to completely cover my eyes because I did not want light to wake me from my sleep.

Light is permeating.

Moses face shone when he spent time in God's presence (Exodus 34:29-35). So much so that it made others around him uncomfortable. Can you imagine what that looked like? Moses had to cover his face with a veil while speaking with the Israelites because his glow was too much for them — they feared his glow.

There are those who don't want to see our light. They're comfortable in their slumber. They know about the Light but they don't want to be awakened. Moses lived under the old covenant where no one could see the light of God and live. We don't.

Jesus told us, "You are the light of the world—like a city on a hilltop that cannot be hidden. No one lights a lamp and then puts it under a basket. Instead, a lamp is placed on a stand, where it gives light to everyone ...," Matthew 5:14-15.

Darkness is merely the absence of light. We don't notice when darkness is missing, however, we totally notice the absence of light. We we need to see something we can shine a light and see clearly.

That's the thing about light. When it shines in darkness it is mutually beneficial to everyone around. It is personal and beautiful and not only illuminates our world but our light is meant to illuminate Jesus to the world around us.

If we have Jesus living inside of us, we have no reason to ever fear, be intimidated or hide because of darkness.

> *"If you follow me, you won't have to walk in darkness, because you will have the light that leads to life." —John 8:12b*

Following Him means making sure we are keeping our light charged — connected to Jesus. We do this like Moses did, by spending time with the Lord so that we become radiant — sending out light; shining or glowing brightly.[2] As light-bearers, we can also recharge at church or in fellowship with other believers, by studying the Word, listening to sermons, or attending Sunday School or small groups.

Yet can we get caught up in thinking that simply going to church is doing "our part"? By only attending church are we being, as Jesus calls us, "the light of the world"? Because I've noticed that most of those living in darkness can be found *outside* of church.

I say most, because I am testimony to the fact that there are people who come to church in need of the Light. But there are millions more who would never step inside a church until they see the Light in a Christian *outside* of church.

We know about the Light — but do we fully embrace what being "light" means? Unless we are shining the light of Jesus in dark places, we aren't using it effectively. Many people will never see the light until you take the Light into their world.

LIGHT REVEALS

Sometimes once we're living in the Light, we want to completley ignore the past. Learned behavior from past hurts had often sent me into "self-protect" mode. Remembering failures and issues once hidden in darkness was uncomfortable. If I wasn't careful, I could brush past light-thirsty people the Lord put right in front of me because I don't want to see darkness.

One day I was listening to a couple of our friends as they were sharing about some darkness they were walking through. As we sat in silence for a moment, The Lord asked me a question.

"How can I break your heart with the things that break My heart, when you won't allow your heart to be broken?"

That hurt — but it was truth.

In my light-in-the-light world, I can get comfortable. It's easier when all you see is light. I don't bump into things. I don't get hurt. Yet sometimes He's revealing darkness right in front of me that needs some of my Jesus light. I am thankful for these moments when His great love helps me to understand I can no longer turn away from what He has revealed … these moments are often when my light is most effective.

> *We also pray that you will be strengthened with all his glorious power so you will have all the endurance and patience you need. May you be filled with joy, always thanking the Father. He has enabled you to share in the inheritance that belongs to his people, who live in the light. For he has rescued us from the kingdom of darkness and transferred us into the Kingdom of his dear Son, who purchased our freedom and forgave our sins.*
> —Colossians 1:11-13

It is our honor and privilege to shine His light through our lives and engage a world that seems utterly dark. He has called us to shine bright. He asks us to love like Him. He set the pattern for us and even gave us the manual.

I read an Instagram post by Christine Caine @propelwomen. In it, she talks about the Light. Her statement hit home with me.

> "The light inside of you will shine that much brighter if there is darkness around you." —Christine Caine

When the spiritual darkness around me seems overwhelming, if I can, I just remember that one light that broke through the darkness in church that morning. Sharing the light He has given me, I can make a difference. And that one light powered by Jesus makes all the difference in the world.

BRIGHT LIGHTS CAN TAKE A BIG CITY

Here's the thing — we don't lose any light by sharing. Sharing doesn't make our light grow dim — in fact, sharing gives our light even bigger impact.

I'm thinking about the Marriott® ballroom near my home where I have attended many, many meetings. It is a beautiful space, so elegant. Every time I'm in the room my focus is captured by the lightsssss. You see, there are about 12 magnificent chandeliers in the ballroom and there are probably 50 individual, gigantic bulbs in each chandelier. Every single bulb is so intense, that one alone would brighten a small, dark room, but together the light they generate is brilliant.

We could get all technical and talk about light switches and varieties of bulbs and dimmers and faders.... or we could wax scientific and talk about refraction and reflection or even photosynthesis, but in the end...

Light. It is ubiquitous.

On a Christmas Tree no one light is more important than any other but together they do this beautiful work. One bulb on the tree would technically be a lit tree, but how bizarre would a Christmas Tree look with just one light?

Yet, even without one teeny, tiny light, entire rooms are completely dark.

If light attracts, how can we only be lights in a room full of light?

> *It's impossible to disappear from you or to ask the darkness to hide me, for your presence is everywhere, bringing light into my night. There is no such thing as darkness with you. The night, to you, is as bright as the day; there's no difference between the two.* —Psalm 139:11-12 TPT

[1] Strong, James. *Strong's Exhaustive Concordance of the Bible*. Abingdon Press, 1890. https://biblehub.com/greek/5457.htm

[2] Copyright © 1987, 2011 by Helps Ministries, Inc.

[3] "radiant". OED Online. September 2020. Oxford University Press. http://www.oed.com/viewdictionaryentry/Entry/7179;jsessionid=61494FA30F6628009908C800D2210718 (accessed September 23, 2020).

[4] Caine, Christine [@propelwomen] (2018, January 21) "The light inside of you will shine that much brighter if there is darkness around you." https://www.instagram.com/p/BeoFxH4Ai0y/?utm_source=ig_web_copy_link

Chapter 13

SHAME OFF

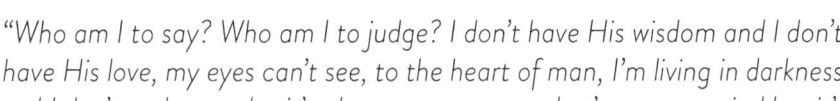

"Who am I to say? Who am I to judge? I don't have His wisdom and I don't have His love, my eyes can't see, to the heart of man, I'm living in darkness and I don't understand... it's always easy to say what's on your mind but it's not always easy to be kind." —Author Unknown

Shame. That familiar sting. The thought that everyone knows about me: what I've done, the choices I've made, how I have failed — over and over. In my early years, those thought patterns caused me to think of myself as a lesser person.

Initially, my shame dated back to childhood but is now, for the most part in my past. There are moments when it tries to rear its ugly head, but just like Wanda said, I now recognize that ugly thing when it tries to insert itself into my thought pattern. I am able to tell it to get lost in Jesus name!

My story is one of great light — that came from a place of great darkness. For many years I've known that when the time was right I was to tell it. Doing that comes with great risk and great joy. When you lay it all out there, someone isn't going to get it. Some are going to miss the point. I keep telling The Lord, "If it's not going to be beneficial to anyone, I don't want to do it." He keeps assuring me that it doesn't matter.

There is great joy in looking back over the altars built in my life. Victories walked out through Jesus love for me.

A tell-all was not what I had in mind. That definitely would help NO ONE. As I began to pray about the project, I spoke with a friend, who is also a counselor, about writing my story. She encouraged me that it was needful and timely. There were a few more friends and colleagues in whom I confided. The book concept definitely resonated with them.

How could I write a book about *The Church* that wouldn't seem like I was throwing the very thing that I love under the bus. I never want to do that. Ever. However I see some things inside *The Church* that are very troubling to my core — and I'm not alone in what I'm seeing.

I'm not a "church-expert". I don't have degrees behind my name and I haven't studied the minute details of ekklesia. But as I have shared; I have experienced an amazing miracle through the Body of Christ — *The Church* — that I know can and should be replicated.

I could not share about my experience with *The Church* without sharing some details of where I have walked. It was inevitable. Reliving some of the darker moments of past so that I can shed light has not been easy. Yet Jesus has brought such healing to my life that I don't have many painful moments regarding shame, though every now and then the residue causes a sting.

Shame. Oh, that no one would ever carry it!

Should Christians ever use the phrase "Shame on you"?

My gut reaction, my heart reaction is NEVER. Wouldn't the better statements be: "Let me show you a more excellent way; Let me introduce you to Jesus; He is how I made it." ?

What made my spiritual transformation so amazing is that I experienced acceptance instead of shame, personal attention instead of gossip, understanding in place of judgment. I had the freedom to stumble and fall while working through my issues.

When I think of the people that we (*The Church*) have shamed over the years because their sin was apparent or their life circumstances made them an easy target, my heart breaks. I am actually crying tears as I write this. I've spoken with many wounded people. My heart is heavy because I know shaming still happens. For some it happens while their shame-r is abusing the "name" of Jesus.

Let that sink in.

Perhaps the sting is real for me because I once lived in my shame. The Lord made a way of escape for me, as He has for us all, but I had people, lining the escape path. People living out their calling as *The Church* walked me out of the cage, pointing me toward The Door[1] and into a relationship with Jesus that forever changed my life.

Early on, even though I was surrounded by encouragers, it wasn't easy. For instance, I felt the sting the first time I walked back into the church building. The first time I walked back onto my old campus I felt the stares. Those stares could have simply been that people were trying to place me, but the enemy of my soul used those whispers against me, trying to make me live in shame.

Shame kept me from going back to college and getting my degree because I didn't want to deal with the fallout of how I left there. Shame kept me from friendships I could have pursued, but I was afraid they would find out the "real me". Shame closed my mouth from talking openly about my restoration for many years because I would have to reveal my past. Shame … it has no place in our vernacular.

> *Those who look to him for help will be radiant with joy; no shadow of shame will darken their faces.* —Psalm 34:5

PERSPECTIVE

I posed this question to my family at lunch one day: "Should a Christian ever use the words 'Shame on you?'"

There were very different answers around the table… my son just looked at me, as he often does when I pose those types of questions, but it wasn't because he thought I was crazy. He was thinking. He's like me… we are thinkers. We revisited the conversation and Devin shared his heart. To shame someone would mean that we are judging them. As Jesus followers, aren't we supposed to refrain judging?

My sweet Ashley's answer was almost immediate. She has thought about this before, as people who have fought an uphill battle with shame do. She said a most definite, "No." She began to share her heart. This topic is one she is very passionate about.

David's knee-jerk reaction was that the only place a word like shame ever belongs is describing those who harm children and innocent people — only as far as it would keep them from repeating those actions.

We had a long, passion-filled discussion, which took up most of our lunch. I wish I would have recorded that conversation because I loved hearing my family's insight and their heart for others. I am blessed.

I have also been blessed on my life's journey and even in writing this book to discover several others who came to know a loving Savior through this beautiful entity called, *The Church*. Some have long since been a part and have been able to move beyond shame to become a thriving member of this body. Some are still on that journey — but each of them have given me the privilege of sharing pieces of their story with you.

FRANNI

*Are not five sparrows sold for two pennies?
And not one of them is forgotten before God.
Why, even the hairs of your head are all numbered.
Fear not; you are of more value than many sparrows.
—Luke 12:6–7 NKJV*

I always knew I was adopted. As a young girl, that fact didn't give me comfort — it taunted me: perhaps because I had such a strained relationship with my mother; perhaps it was because I never felt like I belonged — anywhere. I didn't look like anyone or act like anyone in my adoptive family.

My mother never hugged me or told me that she loved me. I remember thinking, *There must be something very wrong with me to never be touched.* I constantly felt like I was a visitor in my home. Our relationship was very toxic. She resented me and I knew it. I was constantly reminded that she had given up a baby when she was younger.

"We never wanted you," she would say. "I just had to replace the mistake I made. I don't even want to look at you." I believe that she resented since me the day she brought me home. So much so that she would drug me to keep me calm and emotionless. That way she wouldn't have to deal with me.

I was often so jealous of my friends who had those picture perfect mother-daughter relationships.

Why couldn't I have that? I wondered.

Seeds were planted in those formative years. I was never enough. I was unlovable. I was ugly. I was fat. I was dumb. I was a mistake. I grew up being such a follower, just wanting someone to love me.

Someone has to love me, right?

I made horrible decisions when choosing friends. I ended up in juvenile hall for shoplifting as a result of those friend choices, but at least I belonged. I was part of a group. A part of *something*. Those relationships, me following those who made me feel like I belonged, resulted in three years of hardcore bullying. I spent most my time in the bathroom crying, but at least I was being noticed. I kept getting myself in trouble — at home, at school, in life.

All of these circumstances lead me to some very dark places. My thoughts were haunted with ways to take my life. I didn't want to live the existence I knew. I often thought of ways to make my exit, but would never follow through.

Then one day everything changed. I met a girl named Tammy who invited me to church. I wasn't really a church-goer. I grew up Catholic and would go to mass on Christmas and maybe Easter, but I wanted Tammy to like me so I decided to go with her. I'm not sure I really realized how much, but that day my whole world changed.

The church was SO FRIENDLY. That really, really, really, freaked me out. I mean REALLY FREAKED ME OUT. Everyone was hugging everyone else! On top of that, they were telling each other, "I love you!"

"It must be drugs," I told Tammy.

She rolled her eyes as she was used to my sarcastic comments masking any feelings that were deep or real. Self protection. I was good at it.

Then, this little elderly woman hugged me during the church's fellowship time and said "I sure do love you." I pushed her away hard and said, "Lady, you don't even know me." Tammy was so embarrassed — I could see her face.

The little elderly woman surprised me. She said, "You are right, I do not know you, but I know God, the God who created this beautiful girl standing in front of me and He loves you and I love Him." I felt a whole bunch of feelings I had never felt before! My eyes welled up with tears. I didn't know what to say so I quickly excused myself to the restroom. I remember that night. I could not stop crying and it wasn't a sad, woe is me cry. For the first time I just felt so loved. That deep Jesus love. At the time I still didn't know what was happening, but from that moment on I longed to and did spend the majority of time at this church. It was magic to me.

Once I got over being totally freaked out, I got really involved in the youth group. I met the youth pastor and his wife and I just thought she walked on water. She was so kind and loving and she *noticed me*. Her name is Wilma and she took me under her wing. I didn't know it then but God had placed her in my life. Not only did she show me a mother's love but she helped me learn how to receive that love so I would be able to know Him and begin the healing in my life. She was my Jesus with skin.

Back then I hated to be hugged. I winced, flinched and had this repulsive look on my face, like I was in so much pain, death was imminent. I hated to be told, "I love you." My auto-response was always, "Yeah, yeah, you too."

Wilma hugged me often and I would always try to pull away. She would say, "I'm not letting you go until you hug me back." And she didn't. Sometimes we would be standing there for 10-15 minutes, her holding me so tightly while my arms hung limp. This ritual went on for at least a year and I knew that sometimes I drove her crazy. I was difficult, I was moody, I was broken. But she never let go first. She never gave up on me.

I remember the first time I hugged her back, I melted and I broke. She prayed such a beautiful prayer over me. I will never forget it. She just kept repeating the name of Jesus in such a tender way. It was in those sweet moments at church that I discovered a loving, faithful, never-lying God, who cared that much about me and the pain I buried so deeply in my heart. I was forever changed.

VINCE

It is my nature to be wordy. Unnecessarily expanding on things that can be easily communicated and understood in a quick sentence. I'm a hairdresser what can I say? For that reason I am intentionally going to keep this short and to the point.

I was not raised in a "Christian" home or with any sort of faith upbringing. My parents are simple, decent people as were those who introduced me to Christ.

My childhood was not without its challenges, some of which I'll never allow in print for the sake of collateral damage. My mother is on her fourth marriage to a man she married while he was in prison for attempted murder. My father is on his third marriage and I have nine siblings between them. My parent's substance abuse, my stepparents, inappropriate situations, questions about my identity and sexuality — were all part of my adolescent sparring. No need for details — this should give you enough of a start to imagine what challenges may have been presented.

Moving forward I will say this, from the moment I accepted the salvation that Jesus freely offers to all, I have boldly known that God has my back and that I walk in divine favor and protection. My life was radically transformed in one moment. I went from fearing the future and a genuine sense of hopelessness to hope overflowing. Peace in an instant replaced overwhelming unworthiness and self doubt.

My life is richly blessed and I am certain this is because I am hidden in Christ. I run a very successful salon business and have two amazing daughters who all but worship me. I'm married to my absolute best friend and have been successfully married for almost 13 years. We live in a premier community in our city and are surrounded by absolute salt of the earth people on every side of us. Our friendships are deep and my clients treat me and my family like we are their own. I want for nothing.

The extravagant love of Father God is so evident in my life that it's been a topic of conversation among my workmates and I am not unaware of the witness my life is to those secretly watching. I could just as easily detail the accounts of blessing as I could have the struggles but I've given enough to fill in the gaps.

I can remember as a kid feeling helpless to change or control any part of what my life looked like and that helplessness overwhelmed me. I knew I didn't want to live a life like my parents, but felt powerless to manifest any other reality. When I heard the Good News of Jesus after being invited to church at the age of 16; that there was a God who loved me and cared for me and wanted to know me, I accepted that love and care — no questions asked no holds barred.

I'm almost thankful I wasn't raised "in church" because I've never seen God as anything but a Rescuer... truly a Savior, a Safe Place, a Refuge. Devouring his Word, learning what the scriptures have to say about my life has been truly transforming.

I'll finish with this: Life is going to kick you in the teeth, and for some of us it will be more than once or twice. But Jeremiah 29:11 has been a promise well kept in my life and I have nothing but gratitude and praise to show for it. I am glad that in the hard things of this life I have a place of refuge (Psalm 91) and peace in knowing that there is a God who's concerned with me and a Savior who covers me. This is my testimony. God is good and his promises are true.

AMBERLY

It's hard for someone like me to describe what the love of God truly means. If I am being honest with myself, for many reasons when I was younger I felt every right to disprove anyone can love or even be loved. I would like to be able to say that I have figured it all out; that I understand God and "the church". However, I cannot say that I understand. Seeing so much hate and control, I'm not sure we are meant to fully understand the complexity of this life we are given. As I've grown, my understanding of love has matured. It's still hard to describe, but I can give it my best try.

Growing up I identified as atheist. Many factors played a role in that, too many to delve into. It's complicated, as I have come to find out many things are. But I have found one simple truth, no matter what religion I identify as, my most basic human need is love — to be loved.

If you hit the fast-forward button on my life starting from birth going into young adulthood, you would learn what "someone like me" means. You would see a child silently begging for help, her bright big eyes telling you everything you need to know, if only someone would have just taken the time to stop and look. You would hear screams of innocence. You would see tears heavy with sadness of someone else's burden. You would get to understand that "someone like me" was in need of love — and not the kind you pay a price for.

The thing I was pleading for the most and the one that tends to be the root of many issues that surface in my walk of healing, is the love of a mother. I am happy to spoil the ending of that story — I eventually found that love in God. Strange to describe that I found the one thing I have been searching for — the love of a mother — in God who is usually depicted as masculine. But for me, my God gives me the love of kindness and gentleness that typically feels very feminine.

When I finally ended up in a physical church setting I was a 20-year-old critic. I didn't trust and my defensive walls did not care who they hurt in the process of protecting myself. I do have regrets. I wish I had not been so externally rigid. I didn't mean to push people away. It was just my way of coping with my trauma. I understand now that I can do that in a kinder way towards others and more importantly towards myself.

Church was a strange place for "someone like me". I learned rather quickly that some of the things I knew I hated — like smiling, hugging, talking to strangers, asking questions, to name a few — "church people" did every Sunday morning. I tried to distance myself from others in the beginning of my first few weeks in attendance. I wasn't there to meet new people, I was there to learn more about this God everyone seemed to be so in love with.

I soon learned that many people attend church for what I would say are for the wrong reasons. They do not come to find God; they come to see their friends. They do not come to learn more about God, but to learn more about everyone else's lives and insert themselves into peoples business. They judge, lie, and create an unrealistic view of what their life looks like, when truly they are broken and hurting on the inside— some are even unaware that this is what they're portraying.

However, that is only one side of "the church". I've come to find that there is good and bad everywhere, even in a church setting. In the beginning of my church experience I had a hard time trying to un-focus on the bad. It was always front and center. It was much harder for me to find the good, but once I found it I could not un-see it. That love I had been searching for I found through God's people and eventually found it in God.

I came in to my first church as that 20-year-old broken young person and left much stronger and whole. The love of some of those people changed my life. And it wasn't just the love they expressed in words; it was the love their actions proved time and time again, which for someone who was let down repeatedly while growing up, meant so much more than anything someone could say out of their mouth. Their actions proved what words sometimes could not. After all a critic is hard to convince. But as love was shown to me, I began to trust.

Some of those acts of love were so selfless. They opened a door of vulnerability; sometimes even crossing boundaries that probably looking back should have been more respected. I try not to dwell on that, but it's hard not to. I've now learned about my own boundaries too. What I want that to look like and how to implement those boundaries in a healthy way. I am proud of my growth through those hard, challenging times.

I remember when my college professor first invited me to a church service. She didn't have to, but she did.

I remember when a family at church allowed me, for a much-needed season, to be one of their own. They didn't have to, but they did.

I remember when my pastor let me share a part of my story on a Sunday morning with the church. He didn't have to, but he did.

I remember when I was homeless and someone from church got me into a program that allowed me to have my own apartment. She didn't have to, but she did.

I remember when a woman designated time out of her incredibly busy schedule just for me whenever I needed it. She didn't have to, but she did.

And I remember finally understanding that God will always and forever be there for me. God doesn't have to be, but is everything I will always need. My relationship with God is the only thing that has no ability to hurt me or let me down in the process. So when I think back on the bad, I now understand a key part on how to overcome the darkness — is love. And for "someone like me"— love is everything.

SHAME OFF US

A common thread weaves it's way through my friend's stories as well as my own: God uses imperfect people from an imperfect church to share His perfect love.

The love of Christ neutralizes shame.

A few years ago, Christine Caine wrote a book called, *UNASHAMED: Drop Your Baggage, Pick Up Your Freedom, Fulfill Your Destiny*. She captured the heart of many and exposed shame's game. Her writings, including *UNASHAMED*, have helped people like me know that we are not alone in our experiences or our life-journeys. I highly recommend reading it, especially if you are in walking this process out.

Jesus disarmed our shame on the cross. His love causes shame to release its grip on the hearts, minds and lives of humanity.

And He chose us, *The Church*, to be the conduit of that love.

SHAME OFF

¹The Door is Jesus, as He calls Himself in John 10:7-9. Strongs G 2374, thyra, meaning a portal or entrance.

²https://www.proverbs31.org/read/devotions/full-post/2016/09/13/shame-off-you

Chapter 14

GOD IS FOR US

CHRISTIANS, PHARISEES & SINNERS, OH MY!

One of the best things to come about in 2020[1] is the song, *The Blessing*[2] — it is simple, yet profound. Its truth has been a comfort during this tumultuous time in our country and around the world.

Taken from Numbers 6:24-26, the song pronounces blessing, the same priestly blessing that the Lord gave to Aaron and his sons (through Moses) to bless the Israelites.

> *The Lord bless you and keep you;*
> *the Lord make his face shine on you*
> *and be gracious to you;*
> *the Lord turn his face toward you*
> *and give you peace.*
> *—Numbers 6:24-26 NIV*

How cool is it that the Lord God wanted to bless His people? He wanted to bless Israel so much, that He gave His own blessing to be passed on and passed down. If you know Jesus, you're His people too!

This priestly blessing of Aaron has been heard by many people, even if they don't realize or understand its origin. The passage is often used as the benediction in church services, in Christian schools — even at funerals.

The Blessing anthem is beautifully written and easily singable, beginning quietly with a solemn pronouncement of Numbers 6:24-26 followed by strong affirmation as the chorus rings with a resounding, "Amen! (So be it)." The next part of the song, the bridge, carries this personal blessings to a-whole-nother level. Every time we sing this song, I am overjoyed to pronounce this blessing over people. Some may not understand or grasp God's favor, but everyone can understand this simple truth: He is with you! He is for you!

There is no more powerful thought or concept in the world: that the God of the universe is for you! The song was meant to be sung to others. Before the pandemic really took hold in the States we asked our congregation to literally get our of their seats and sing this part to other people. *The Blessing* was meant to be given.

Yet — do we get to choose who receives this blessing? Aren't we supposed to bless those who curse us (Luke 6:28). How hard is that?

ZACCHAEUS

Zacchaeus was a tax collector, hated by his fellow Jews. Historically, tax collectors were Jews working for Rome to enforce heavy taxation which also allowed them to bilk their fellow Jews for more than they owed. Right in front of everyone, Jesus called Zacchaeus out — but not in the way one would think. The Bible says:

> *Jesus entered Jericho and made his way through the town. There was a man there named Zacchaeus. He was the chief tax collector in the region, and he had become very rich. He tried to get a look at Jesus, but he was too short to see over the crowd. So he ran ahead and climbed a sycamore-fig tree beside the road, for Jesus was going to pass that way. When Jesus came by, he looked up at Zacchaeus and called him by name. "Zacchaeus!" he said. "Quick, come down! I must be a guest in your home today." Zacchaeus quickly climbed down and took Jesus to his house in great excitement and joy. But the people were displeased. "He has gone to be the guest of a notorious sinner," they grumbled.* —Luke 19:1-7

Here's the thing: Jesus blessed Zacchaeus with His presence BEFORE salvation was even a consideration in Zacchaeus' mind, life or home. Jesus didn't accuse him. Jesus didn't call out all of his wrongdoings in front of everyone. Jesus didn't bring him up on trial. Jesus met him where he was. Jesus was *for* Zacchaeus.

Jesus was kind to "sinners". Jesus was a friend of "sinners". Jesus loved, loves and is loving towards "sinners". He wants the opportunity to show grace so that "sinners" will know that He really *is* for them. He wants people to receive healing, to be reconciled to the Father, to live an abundant live with Him, to be saved from a vicious hell.

By loving or blessing a "sinner", we're not winking at their sin. Jesus didn't get to know

> **SIDE NOTE**
>
> I recently learned of a Casting Crowns song written several years ago by Mark Hall and Matthew West. The song, called *Jesus Friend of Sinners*,[3] is gripping. I can't listen to it or even read the lyrics without weeping.
>
> See MUSIC NOTES at the end of this chapter so that you can find the song on YouTube or in iTunes. The chorus so masterfully states what my writing is trying to convey.

people and then leave them without confronting their sin, but He also didn't start off by judging them. He met them — He met me — He meets us — where we are.

When we love those trapped in sin or circumstances or their normal or seemingly natural way of life, when we meet their felt needs, we have a greater opportunity to introduce them to Jesus.

Jesus ministered to people who didn't know Him as Savior. He met them at their greatest point of need. The Bible says He healed, fed and delivered complete strangers from all walks of life. He had compassion on everyone. He saw beyond the obvious. Just like when I was trapped in my sin and dysfunction, I didn't have to get myself together before He rescued me. In fact, it was obvious that I couldn't — but I cried out to the Lord right where I was and He met me.

Zacchaeus had a need to see Jesus. So much so that he climbed a tree just to get a glimpse. Jesus took it next level and went to Zacchaeus' home — much to the chagrin of the onlookers, Jesus showed love for him.

> *Meanwhile, Zacchaeus stood before the Lord and said, "I will give half my wealth to the poor, Lord, and if I have cheated people on their taxes, I will give them back four times as much!"*
> *Jesus responded, "Salvation has come to this home today, for this man has shown himself to be a true son of Abraham. For the Son of Man came to seek and save those who are lost." —Luke 19:8-9*

Jesus very presence changed Zacchaeus' life. He was for Zacchaeus. He didn't stand with those who were against Zacchaeus. He didn't stand with Zacchaeus in his sin. He simply showed Zacchaeus a more excellent way.

I DON'T TAKE SIDES

One morning during a time of worship the Lord spoke very plainly to me. He said, "I don't take sides."

That statement seemed sort of random, yet I clearly heard Him. Not knowing exactly what He meant in that moment, I began searching my brain's database for instances in my own life of side-taking — supporting one person or opinion over another. A few thoughts came to mind.

One of those thoughts had to do with the proverbial mask wars during the pandemic. In case you weren't aware of these wars, there was great division between those who were strong, pro mask wearers and those who felt strongly against wearing a mask. While I could not judge anyone for their personal belief or conviction, there were those who were very vocal, each speaking negatively about the "other side".

So in that moment that morning, I wondered if the Lord was telling me not to take a side in that war and perhaps He was, but the words He spoke wouldn't leave me.

Little did I know He was taking me on a journey to understand more about His great love.

At a real loss, I began to seek His heart. Some of my first thoughts were simple, like: *choosing a relationship with the Lord is choosing a side, right? I know He loves everyone and longs for a relationship with everyone, but if people don't choose Him, aren't they still "choosing" a side?*

In our culture and for many generations we are taught, even programmed that life is all about taking sides: good vs. evil; the left vs. the right; the Rebels vs. the Empire — even with kickball in grade school. Choosing a side is programmed in our brain and can become a filter through which we see the world. An "us against them" mentality.

Have we, as Christians, ever taken sides against "sinners"? Have there ever been times that you were so offended by someone's actions or sin that you looked at them with disdain? Talked about them to others? Even cursed them by saying, "They'll never change"? I don't want to admit it, but I have done that. I have looked at others as if being a Christian gave me the right to be against them.

> *Are you really showing true love by only loving those who love you back? Even those who don't know God will do that. Are you really showing compassion when you do good deeds only to those who do good deeds to you? Even those who don't know God will do that.* —Luke 6:32-33 TPT

This us against them mentality causes us to lose sight that on the other "side" is a flawed human being — just like us. Possibly a person who needs to be introduced to Jesus. How can we ever have the hope of doing that if we can get past what we see?

Even those of us who love the Lord can look at ourselves and our relationship with the Lord this way. If we're good, He is on our side. If we're bad, He is against us.

Listening to a podcast one afternoon, the speaker read a passage in Joshua that began to open my understanding of what the Lord was saying to me about taking sides. "... While Joshua was there near Jericho: He looked up and saw right in front of him a man standing, holding his drawn sword. Joshua stepped up to him and said, 'Whose side are you on—ours or our enemies'?' He said, 'Neither. I'm commander of GOD's army,'" Joshua 5:13-14a, MSG.

> *"Whose side are you on—ours or our enemies'?"*
> *He said, "Neither. I'm commander of GOD's army."*

I had never really looked at that passage this way. The commander of God's army wasn't there to take a side, even though he had his sword drawn. His purpose for being there was to do the will of God — to see to it that God's commands were followed and carried out.

The Commander of the Lord's army was saying, "I am here to do the will of The Lord. Period."

I kept praying, reading and seeking the Lord about taking sides. I wanted to fully understand. I dug into the gospels trying to remember examples where Jesus took someone's side.

A few days later while reading in Matthew 11, specifically part of verse 29 leapt out at me:

> *"Let me teach you, because I am humble and gentle at heart..."*

Of all verses to speak about not taking sides. Yet my heart literally pounded as He began to teach me. I continued to read. He was showing me Himself.

MY STREAM

I began contemplating how Jesus was and is the most humble One to ever grace the earth — yet He had all authority. ALL. I started remembering how, even though He had all authority and He could have had God punch the smite button[4] on any one at any time, He chose to "do the will of Him who sent me..." John 6:38, NIV. I thought about how many times He said those words throughout the gospels. He was about His Father's business.

> *"...I carry out the will of the one who sent me, not my own will,"*
> *—John 5:30*

Then I recalled how Jews of that day wanted Jesus to take their side. If He really was the Messiah, He was their ticket to freedom. In their understanding, the freedom He would bring would decimate the Roman empire, freeing them from hundreds of years of captivity. After all, in past times, God had delivered them by decimating their enemies.

But God was doing a new thing. Something unheard of — a stream in the desert.

Once and for all Jesus brought everlasting freedom to ALL humankind.

The Father wanted it to be the way it was supposed to be in the beginning. He wanted to have relationship with us and Jesus, the Ultimate Sacrifice, was the only way that could happen. Isn't that why Jesus came — to do the will of the Father?

> *This is how much God loved the world: He gave his Son, his one and only Son. And this is why: so that no one need be destroyed; by believing in him, anyone can have a whole and lasting life. God didn't go to all the trouble of sending his Son merely to point an accusing finger, telling the world how bad it was. He came to help, to put the world right again. Anyone who trusts in him is acquitted; anyone who refuses to trust him has long since been under the death sentence without knowing it. And why? Because of that person's failure to believe in the one-of-a-kind Son of God when introduced to him. —John 3:16-18 MSG*

So, what about the Pharisees? Wasn't Jesus against them? I pointed to Scripture in earlier chapters that Jesus spent time with sinners, and this included the Pharisees. He went to synagogue, He talked with them often as they frequently questioned His every move. On occasion, He even ate with them. Although it seemed as though He was against the Pharisees and other teachers of the law, His direct words were actually attempts to bring them to the truth of who He was. Some, like Nicodemus heard Jesus loud and clear, giving up position, rank and status to follow Him.

Jesus never took sides. He was and is for all humankind. He came to seek and save all who were and are lost. He continues to reach for all of us, not willing that a single person would miss out. His heart is that everyone would choose the freedom His love brings.

He's not interested in taking a side on the things that would seek to divide us. He didn't come to correct our politics, religious rules or personal arguments. He didn't come to pick a favorite religious denomination or leader. His plan was not to set Christians against "sinners". He said it plainly. He came to "seek and save those who are lost". He invites us to follow His example. He is for us! He is with us!

AM I A FRIEND OF SINNERS?

There are some people in my life right now who I need to spend more time with. We have made fast friends, but I don't really know them that well. For instance, I don't know if they have ever been introduced to Jesus. If not, I hope I get make that introduction. I want to tell them how Jesus changed my life. Not because they are bad people, but because Jesus loves them. Everyone needs Jesus. Every single one.

Traditional thinking tells me that my people are going straight to hell and that I should stay away. Jesus says, "I love them. You love them too."

It's not hard for me to love these people in my life. They are lovable.

What about those who aren't easily lovable? What about the Zacchaeus' in our lives? Will we bless them with the same love? Will I? Will you?

[1] The best "thing" that happened for David and me in 2020 was the birth of our grandson: Samuel Ezra Chaney.

[2] Songwriters: Chris Brown / Steven Furtick / Cody Carnes / Kari Brooke Jobe
The Blessing lyrics © Worship Together Music, Capitol Cmg Paragon, Be Essential Songs, Kari Jobe Carnes Music, Writers Roof Publishing

[3] Songwriters: Matthew West / Matthew Joseph West
Jesus, Friend of Sinners lyrics © Sony/atv Tree Publishing, Songs Of Southside Independent Music Publishing, Songs For Delaney, My Refuge Music, Atlas Holdings, One77 Songs

[4] Author: Gary Larson, ©1987, The Far Side. The smite button is reference to a Far Side cartoon, where God's finger is hovering over a computer keyboard right above a key displaying the word "smite".

MUSIC NOTES, CH 14:

Find *The Blessing* on YouTube here: https://youtu.be/Zp6aygmvzM4 or in iTunes at: https://music.apple.com/us/album/the-blessing-live/1509359406?i=1509359412

Find *Jesus Friend of Sinners* on YouTube here: https://youtu.be/BY6VAy9y_iQ or in iTunes at: https://music.apple.com/us/album/jesus-friend-of-sinners/470669414?i=470669424

Chapter 15

BEHIND THE VEIL

AMBER ALERT — A MISSING GENERATION

According to research from Barna president, David Kinnaman's the number of de-churched 18-29 year-olds has increased from 59% in 2011 to 64% in 2019.[1]

Numbers from Lifeway Research[2] are equally startling. In 2017, 69% of young adults say they were attending at age 17. That number fell to 58% at age 18 and 40% at age 19.

These statistics from Barna and Lifeway, while a few digits apart, are strikingly close. They reflect what I have seen throughout my years in ministry. Maybe you've witnessed this de-churching too.

David and I have had the privilege of working at a few different churches in our 30+ years of ministry, none of them quite the same. Yet there is a commonality we have noticed — as the years have gone by, many church "young people" have walked out the door after High School and don't see a reason to come back.

Sometimes they are simply working out their own salvation with fear and trembling, trying to figure out why they believe, what they believe. I get that. As long as they have a solid foundation, they should be seeking the Lord for themselves. But what if they don't?

There are a myriad of reasons why people from any generation are hesitant to be a part of *The Church*. I have spoken with people who have had vastly different church experiences from mine. There are those who don't want to return because of pain they experienced there. It was supposed to be a safe place, yet they were met with cruelty and judgment or even worse, abuse.

Still others had needs — questions, home-life crises, a missing mom or a dad — that went unnoticed because they didn't know how to ask for help. Quite possibly they didn't even know they needed help, because they only knew the "normal" they lived in.

A few broken-hearted people see no relevance in the particular churches they were raised in because it became all about rules and regulations and walking a tightrope that no one can master. Some even wonder if they were raised in a cult.

> *You have died with Christ, and he has set you free from the spiritual powers of this world. So why do you keep on following the rules of the world, such as, "Don't handle! Don't taste! Don't touch!"?* **Such rules are mere human teachings about things that deteriorate as we use them.** *These rules may seem wise because they require strong devotion, pious self-denial, and severe bodily discipline. But they provide no help in conquering a person's evil desires.* —Colossians 2:20-22

"Human teachings that deteriorate as we use them" have often put distance between *The Church* and our now de-churched community. It's as if there is a missing generation — those who were raised in *The Church* yet now want no part of it. De-churched kids are now raising unchurched kids and the cycle is perpetuating.

Why?

In this age of information that is literally at our fingertips every moment of every day, is it possible that we are seeing a generation, maybe two, that believe seeking the Lord is no longer needed or relevant?[3]

That possibility alone makes me want to tell my story now more than ever. I want to speak the truth in love, telling others about the truth of my Jesus.

I have cited research done by others and stated reasons above from people I have personally interviewed but I still question: *Why are people leaving The Church?*

OWNING IT

Authenticity is a word that is spoken a lot these days, sometimes it gets thrown around a little much. I have thought about this word in light of *The Church* and I wonder: Have we missed out on some opportunities to share the goodness of God in our lives when it means showing personal moments of weakness, doubt or sin?

Have we overlooked teaching moments that reveal our need for Him?

Have we refused to live authentically in front of others because we fear failure or rejection?

As a teacher and a worship leader I have missed moments that allowed others to see that I stumble and sometimes fail. Period. What's more, I missed revealing that even in spite of those moments, there is a God who loves, corrects and redeems me — through it all. This is especially important to those who are young in their faith. They need to see real.

Instead there have been times when I filled those teaching moments with a lot of "dos & don't s". I remember my parents telling us when we were small, "Do as I say, not as I do!" I think sometimes this expression can filter into our thinking. For whatever reason, we *The Church* have a hard time showing our humanity. We give people the Word without the why — the power of our testimony — the testimony of how great and awesome and loving and redemptive our God really is.

There comes a point where that reasoning — "Do as I say, not as I do," — doesn't add up anymore. When young people start living their life for real, fighting their own battles, if we haven't shown them real life, they aren't equipped to face the onslaught by knowing that Jesus is in their corner. They can mistakenly think they have to be perfect in order for Jesus to pay any attention at all.

For me, the joy and the sorrow of owning my own crap has been both exhilarating and terrifying.

There is so much freedom in our truth-telling, but it is hard to be real. No one wants to admit to their failures — it's daunting! For. So. Many. Reasons. But if we know Jesus we have the opportunity to glorify Him, His goodness and His great love through *every* part of our lives.

THE WORD WITHOUT THE WHY

As a parent I've missed those moments of authenticity too.

In my early days of parenting, I didn't want Devin to know anything about my past, ever. David and I were determined that Devin would not make the same mistakes we did, one, because he'd never know about them... LOL... and two, he was prayed over while in the womb, breaking every generational curse I could think of and then some! We tried to take every precaution so that his life would be totally free from any of the pain we experienced.

It was a while before I realized that all of my attempts at "protecting" him were actually not helping him. I needed to let him see the real me, struggles and all.

When Devin was young I would try to tell him about God's goodness to me, but there were things in my past that he wasn't mature enough to hear about. There were times that I would try telling him snippets without details — but I was giving him the Word without my why. To a kid, this can begin to sound preachy and unrealistic.

The Lord began dealing with me concerning talking to Devin about my past. I DID NOT WANT TO DO THIS, but I started praying about it, asking for the right opportunity and the right words.

David and I weren't the best at it, but we tried to each spend quality time with Devin. Mom & Devin days were the best. Sometimes Devin and I would see a movie or go to a game store and we always found something to eat. I appreciated him giving me that time, even the days that ended up being a shopping trip for things he needed. It was my good pleasure to spend time with him and meet his needs.

One particular Mom & Devin day though, is forever etched in my mind. We grabbed a bite to eat at Panera Bread® and Holy Spirit whispered, "It's time." I wasn't expecting to hear that... but He is Good and I trust Him.

So, I jumped in. As authentically as I could, I opened up about my past, with lots of tears on my part. In order for Devin to better grasp the reality that God is for him — no matter what — he had to know that God was for me, even in my failures. In order to share my victories with Devin, he had to hear about my life — events, mistakes and even the pain.

What ended up being an entire afternoon was actually an opening into a truthful place. It was so hard to open up to my son, but so worth it. There were more conversations and questions to come and I sure didn't dump my whole life at once. Yet I was able to demonstrate real life and a real God by sharing what He's done for me.

After sharing so much personal information about his momma, I asked Devin how he felt about me. He said to me, "Not one thing has changed, Mom."

It wasn't that I needed to confess to him all of my shortcomings and failures, but I needed to reveal to my son the redemptive nature of God in my own life. Those struggles will come for Devin. They come for each us and the word of our testimony, coupled with the Word, is living proof that God is Good.

If God did it for me, He will do it for Devin and for anyone else. If I simply say, "He's taken care of me, He'll take care of you," and don't share why I can say that with calm assurance, I'm not giving him the full picture. My words my seem empty. I needed to be willing to share the process.

I GET IT

I get trying to protect our kids from our past so that they don't experience all the pain that we have experienced, but where did that thought come from? Isn't that a little backwards? There is so much power in sharing our why.

> *O my people, listen to my instructions.*
> *Open your ears to what I am saying,*
> *for I will speak to you in a parable.*
> *I will teach you hidden lessons from our past*
> *—stories we have heard and known,*
> *stories our ancestors handed down to us.*
> *We will not hide these truths from our children;*
> *we will tell the next generation about the*
> *glorious deeds of the Lord,*
> *about his power and his mighty wonders.*
> *—Psalm 78:1-4*

They need to know and understand God and His word. The most powerful example we can share is how God has revealed Himself to us —in our own lives.

Have we really "protected" our own by not allowing them to see the truth? Could the purpose of our pain be lost in our own vagueness?

WHEN IT COMES TO THE CHURCH

What about when it comes to *The Church*, have we protected our kids from seeing behind the veil in our churches? When they become young adults and begin to see life through their own lens, are they seeing discrepancies? Imperfections? Hypocrisy?

Are they seeing the institution — rather than the mission of — *The Church*?

There is tension between the two. I've known parents, and truthfully, I was one, who gave way more time to the institution of the church rather than being *The Church*. The affect this has on our own children can be disillusioning for them. Kids see one parent, maybe both, fully engaged in serving the institution of the church, while they are starving for their parent's attention and affection. The Lord doesn't ask us to abandon our families or to drag them along in order to serve the institution of the church. He asks us to lead our children on this journey of being *The Church*.

> *And you must love the Lord your God with all your heart, all your soul, and all your strength. And you must commit yourselves wholeheartedly to these commands that I am giving you today.* **Repeat them again and again to your children. Talk about them when you are at home and when you are**

on the road, when you are going to bed and when you are getting up. Tie them to your hands and wear them on your forehead as reminders. Write them on the doorposts of your house and on your gates.
—Deuteronomy 6:5-9

At church I found my tribe, yet there are others where church was a place of wounding. Their greatest hurts were at the hands of church people. The institution, the bad actors, the sheep in wolves clothing — not the Bride of Christ. Behind the veil some of us have not only witnessed unspeakable acts, but are survivors of heinous violence.

Yes, we even have to be willing to speak the truth about these atrocities behind the veil and hold perpetrators accountable.

Otherwise, when our children become young adults, how will they understand the difference between the church, the institution and *The Church*, the Bride of Christ? How can they know God as both loving and just if what they have witnessed in church hasn't been godly?

HARD TRUTH

Recently, someone I love ferociously told me that they were sexually abused at the hands of a person from their church. Mind-blown. As young adult I watched him distance himself from *The Church*. Having been connected to this person the vast majority of my life, I understood some of the reasons why he seemed to hold church and at times, even the Lord, at arm's distance but I didn't fully know the why.

For this, I apologize. I could have pressed, I could have dug deeper, but I didn't.

This act took place when my friend was a child, yet many years later, the struggle is still real. My friend was able to mask the pain for a long while, yet life has a way of bringing up our past, mixing it with other life-challenges and before we know it, we're out of balance and sometimes almost out of control as we try to make sense of the deluge of memories and emotions that wage war against our minds.

My friend doesn't yet realize what a miracle his life displays. He has faced adversity that I can't comprehend. Not only in this area of his life. He has dealt with other major events as well as a virtual lifetime of inequity, yet he is finding help in the midst of it all. God is for him, even though he doesn't currently attend a church.

I don't blame my friend for being skittish about going to church. I pray for his healing. I want to be near as he walks this out with the Lord.

NOW MORE THAN EVER

Another friend recently told me about something termed "faith deconstruction'. I hadn't heard it called this specifically, but it is almost a movement. It consists of systematically pulling apart one's beliefs in order to examine them more closely. My friend however, who in age is a part of this generation that seems to do the most deconstructing, sees a problem. Many of those who deconstruct aren't reconstructing — with the Word, with a mentor, many times not at all.

Now more than ever is the time for us to be real with the next generation. I mean really, really real. Not trying to be hip or to fit in with them, but instead allowing them into our lives, helping them see the real Savior through the real us.

Are we practically living out spiritual disciplines in our lives? Are we not only allowing others to see our dependence upon the Lord, but do our lives lived-out show others how to do the same? Are we willing to take a deep look into the Word and answer honest questions, honestly? Even if we don't know the answer?

> *Don't think you are better than you really are. Be honest in your evaluation of yourselves, measuring yourselves by the faith God has given us.*
> *—Romans 12:3b*

Living honestly and authentically in every area of our lives feels risky, sometimes even fearful, but it can also be God-honoring.

Paul tells Timothy:

> *"Give careful attention to your spiritual life and every cherished truth you teach, for living what you preach will then release even more abundant life inside you and to all those who listen to you," 1 Timothy 4:16 TPT.*

Every generation can make a difference. In the chapter above, Paul tells Timothy, "...don't be intimidated by those who are older than you; simply be the example they need to see by being faithful and true in all that you do. Speak the truth and live a life of purity and authentic love as you remain strong in your faith," (1 Timothy 4:12 TPT).

Let's not look at the past or feel regret for what we haven't done so far. We can "should have" all over ourselves because the truth is, disciple-making has been our mandate for over 2,000 years. But don't look back — look differently. We can repent — turn in the opposite direction — and start looking for opportunities the Lord gives us to invest in others — as we follow Him.

I'm burdened for a generation of former church-goers, those who are now de-churched, both young and old, that not only have moved away from church, but even more who struggle in their relationship with Jesus. We can win their hearts by showing them Jesus heart for us, even in our humanity.

It's time for we, *The Church*, to get real.

It's time for we, *The Church*, to make the purposeful investment into the every generation.

It's time for us to make room for "them" in our hearts, in our lives and in *The Church*.

[1]*https://www.barna.com/research/resilient-disciples/*

[2]*https://blog.lifeway.com/newsroom/2019/01/15/most-teenagers-drop-out-of-church-as-young-adults/*

[3]*According to the Lifeway newsroom article quoted above, many young people don't see The Church as relevant to today's culture. 70% of the those polled in say that they left due to a difference in "religious, ethical or political beliefs."*

Chapter 16

MAKE ROOM

FOR THE NEXT GENERATION OF THE CHURCH

IMAGINE THIS....

The musician energetically runs out from behind the curtain onto the stage almost immediately making the audience a part of his music. The crowd goes wild as he masterfully, seemingly spontaneously brings them into his show. He begins with his voice, singing one note then gesturing for the crowd to join in. They gleefully and willfully respond with great delight, understanding that they are in the presence of a genuine musical virtuoso.

This goes on for several minutes. He gives three different sections of the crowd each a distinct note to sing. Each section of the crowd echoes back their note, until he gives the cue for them to join their notes together. As they sing collectively, building this grand crescendo, the band comes in forcefully on the downbeat and the crowd is thrilled to the point of screaming!

Watching on video wasn't enough — I wanted to be there. I wanted to be in on what the concert master was creating. Even though some of the chords sounded different to me and not necessarily what I would have thought to sing, he was bringing everyone who was willing in on what he was creating. His music was affecting the lives of everyone in the house, even those of us who were later watching by video, like me. We, the audience, came to understand that we were no longer observing — we were now a part of creating something bigger than us all.

Jacob Collier is the musician I reference. He masterfully did and does what so many musicians skip over. I've been to many concerts where the bands make the show all about themselves. The crowds do sing along and they are thrilled to be in the presence of such wonderful music makers, but concert goers leave the venue thinking, *wasn't that great music? What a great band*! When people leave a Jacob Collier concert, they leave having been a part of the master's music. They leave thinking, *I can make music too*! *That "concert" was a moment I'll never forget*!

Perhaps it's good marketing on Jacob's part, but having followed his music for years now, I believe he genuinely wants to create an experience for everyone, freely teaching what he's learned and involving others on his fantastical musical journeys.

ALWAYS WITH THE QUESTIONS

I can't help but think about this experience in light of our Master and the faith-journey we travel with Him.

Do we keep these journey's to ourselves? Or are we involving others, including future generations?

Are we, *The Church*, teaching those within our reach? Allowing them, not only to participate in our adventures, but helping them walk out their own adventure of a lifetime the Master has prepared for just for them?

> *Do not neglect the spiritual gift you received through the prophecy spoken over you when the elders of the church laid their hands on you.*
> *—1 Timothy 4:14*

Are we allowing the next generation to "stir up the gift within" even when their gift doesn't look like ours?

DAVID JOINS THE BAND

My husband, David, comes from a very musical family. I've listened many times as he and his parents reminisce about family gatherings they used to have when David was young. Every time they gathered together the place was filled with music and singing. Aunts, uncles and cousins, from the oldest to the youngest made music. Everyone was included.

Music is second nature to David. He remembers noodling around on the first instrument they had in the house, a second-hand organ. His parents recognized his musical giftedness, so when he began taking an interest in the saxophone at 10-years old, they invested in a good, quality student horn and private lessons.

David continued to develop and with the encouragement of his private lesson instructor, his parents sacrificed and saved to purchase a professional level horn — the horn he still plays to this day. David's parents made sure he had every opportunity to nurture the gift God gave him.

> *Direct your children onto the right path, and when they are older, they will not leave it.* —Proverbs 22:6

The church (my church) his family attended was large and happening. They had a dynamic music ministry, including several choirs, a full rhythm section and even a horn section. It was both inspiring and intimidating for a 12-year-old boy. However when Jimmy (remember Jimmy?) learned that David had been playing the saxophone for two years already, he invited and encouraged David to join the band.

David fondly remembers those early beginnings — he says he couldn't keep up with the notes on the page! At first, he would get lost before the introduction to the song had finished, but no one ever told him to quit. In fact, they encouraged him to stay. There was a young, twenty something gentleman, Mike, who played the trombone.[1] David said that he would sit next to Mike nearly every service as Mike worked patiently with him to help him follow the music set before him.

Once David caught on and was playing well, a new band director came along, Dave. Dave poured himself into the band members, planning outings, taking the band on trips and building unity within the group. Dave helped the band grow, but he did so by investing time into each player and making sure the new members had space to grow.

The band got involved in Teen Talent, a denominational event held every few years. This event gave churches from each local district the opportunity to allow teens to use their gifts. They competed in everything from playing an instrument to singing to writing to dramas to art to Bible quizzing. Individual teens who won in their solo division were offered scholarships to a Bible college. David was a part of that band that got to participate in Teen Talent, which opened up a whole new world of possibilities to him.

David was learning so much, that he began being featured as a soloist on his sax in church services. Though we weren't dating or even thinking about dating, I remember many of those moments. Far more than his skillful playing, people worshiped the Lord as he glorified God with his gift. It was (and still is) amazing to see how his act of worship brings others into the presence of the Lord.

> *Compose new melodies that release new praises to the Lord. Play his praises on instruments with the anointing and skill he gives you. Sing and shout with passion; make a spectacular sound of joy..*
> —Psalm 33:3 TPT

When he was 15, David entered Teen Talent playing his saxophone. He won in our district, then he won in our state, going all the way to nationals. At nationals his world continued to open up as he met other teens who had wonderful gifts in music. Beyond his dreams, David won the national title in the woodwind solo category! It was no shock to all of us looking in from the outside, but that win allowed him to get a full-ride scholarship for his first year of college.

Continuing to pursue the Lord as well as his musical acumen, David taught himself to play the piano. He began playing the keyboard with one of the choirs now and then, which he really enjoyed. Even though he was self taught, the guys in the rhythm section encouraged him and made him a part of what they were doing. One man in particular, Bill, encouraged David consistently. It got to the place where Bill and David gave one another cues and nods and friendship. Bill is still one of David's closest friends and favorite musicians to play music with to this day.

On the keyboards, David began playing with different music groups at church. They ministered in nursing homes, in other churches and at youth camps and other events during the summer.

When it was time for college, David learned of a select traveling group from the Bible college he wanted to attend that was taking auditions for a piano player — not even his main instrument — but he tried out and he got the gig.

He went to his first year of college with a scholarship, his saxophone and a keyboard, and he kept moving forward. I could go on and on about not only his accomplishments, but his heart, his years of ministry and how he serves the Lord.

But it all began in the band — where different people along the way made room for him. They could have rightfully said, *you're not good enough yet*. They could have said, *wait until you get a little more experience under your belt*.

They not only made a place for and were patient with him, they invested in a boy with a horn who wanted to be a part of something bigger.

> *He makes the whole body fit together perfectly. As each part does its own special work, it helps the other parts grow, so that the whole body is healthy and growing and full of love.* —Ephesians 4:16

Years later, David continues to make room for others. Remember Mikey, that I talked about a few chapters back? When we invited him to come to church and be a part of the horn section, Mikey wanted to join so badly but he didn't have a horn. Without hesitation,

David gave Mikey that good, quality student horn and private lessons every week at our house. Mikey grew by leaps and bounds in his playing and his understanding of music theory. When it was time to purchase his own saxophone, David went with Mikey to help him find the perfect fit.

ARE WE MAKING ROOM FOR THEIR GIFTS?

In the last days," God says, "I will pour out my Spirit upon all people. Your sons and daughters will prophesy. Your young men will see visions, and your old men will dream dreams. In those days I will pour out my Spirit even on my servants—men and women alike—and they will prophesy. And I will cause wonders in the heavens above and signs on the earth below...
—Acts 2:17-19a

David's gift was easily accepted by those in *The Church*. Yet there are those individuals we have forfeited because we couldn't help them find their place.

Have you ever heard of a music genre called "Screamo"? My son had a part in this movement with his Christian band, aptly named, Beheading the Beast. If you're unfamiliar with this genre, it is a form of music that involves screaming vocals. Rock music bands infuse scripture with warfare — almost like warring songs for the Kingdom.

Several years ago, my friend William formed a band with several others that ministered through Screamo music. In their church-world this music was new, it was relevant and it was controversial. Church people who heard the sound approached church leadership declaring that because of the guttural cries and the loud, harsh music that it was the devil's worship.

But the band's hearts were pure. They felt the anointing and calling from the Lord to use this music. William even took one of his favorite songs, "Blessed Assurance" and reframed it in this new way, so that perhaps it could relate to both old and new generations. But there were those who even rejected "Blessed Assurance" because it didn't sound like the old — the way it was when they first heard it.

When the band was asked to play for the church's youth retreat — William began warring through the music. The kids at the retreat began to fall on their faces before the Lord in reverence and awe. It was a sovereign move.

Just like David did, William and the band competed in local Teen Talent and won! The judges, who critiqued every band during the competition didn't exactly know what category to place them in. They were so different from the other bands, but they were the clear winners. Other teens attending that competition loved the band because someone dared to speak their language.

The band went to the national competition in San Antonio and gave it their all. They didn't win the competition, but they knew they were there for something more.

Because their music related to a new generation, they were asked to play one song in front of the entire crowd gathered in San Antonio that year — roughly 30,000 people. As they began to play and sing, 5,000 kids ran to the front of the room and danced and jumped and worshiped with William and the band.

For the rest of that week in San Antonio, William and gang were "celebrities", however they understood that God was using them to do something new, fresh and current. Their "Screamo" ministry was bathed in purity of heart.

When they got back home, no one could seem to find a place for William and the band. There was no "church box" for this new, controversial movement. Eventually the band members found other places to use this creative, God-given gift. Unfortunately, it wasn't for *The Church*.

OLD AND NEW

As *The Church*, sometimes we haven't managed or embraced the "and" very well. We can hold our tradition so sacred that we're not realizing, perhaps not understanding, or, I fear, not even caring that we aren't making room for the new.

Their gifts may not look like ours, but as Jesus followers, we are responsible for helping them stir up the gift within.

Tom & Lisa are on our worship ministry team at church — well, Lisa doesn't sing, but she's as much a part of our team as Tom. Their son, Isaiah was getting ready to leave for college. He knew what he wanted to do, but there was some struggle moving towards his dream.

He knew he was called to "ministry" but what he was passionate about and what is known as "typical ministry" didn't seem like they could coexist.

I didn't know about any of this, but while I was praying one day the Lord showed me that Isaiah is a laborer in this last day harvest. I began to share this with Tom and asked what Isaiah was going to major in at college.

Isaiah's calling is unconventional. His scholarship was in E-sports. Ever heard of it? Me neither — but this is a part of his gift. The people he will be able to minister to I could never reach. Isaiah's calling is different, but it's no less a calling than yours or mine.

Part of our responsibility as *The Church* is to help guide the next generation. They need to know and understand God's word. They need to know, understand and learn how to use their individual gifts and calling. And then they need to be allowed the space and opportunity to begin using those gifts and callings from an early age.

This won't be popular, but I think it's time for all the children to experience "Big Church." (Yes, I said it!) Of course they need Sunday School. They need sound, biblical teaching appropriate for their age, but they also need to see church in action. In our services, in our outreach and in our lives.

You play a part. I play a part. Precept upon precept. Line upon line. Layer upon layer. Discipleship with Jesus is lifelong. We learn and we disciple through the Word and the power of Holy Spirit.

GREAT RISK, GREAT REWARD

It's not always an easy thing to do. Making room for others not only takes us out of our "comfortable" but doing so often involves risk.

Sometimes making room involves great risk. When we prayerfully make the investment in another human being, we don't always see it played out in front us, like my husbands.

What if we pour into someone who never matures in their walk with Jesus? But what if we don't? Our obedience in making room and making disciples has nothing to do with the outcome.

I have witnessed this beautiful cycle through the life of my husband and many others. I thank the Lord that He uses us and allows us to be in on what He is doing. I want all of the investments I make to yield a great return — but sometimes I don't get to see it — and it hurts.

Elijah made room for Elisha. Paul made room for Timothy. Jesus made room for his disciples, including Judas (Iscariot). I'm simplifying, but sometimes we give in obedience and it still hurts.

Isn't that when we're being most like Jesus?

---

[1] *Mike is my cousin and one of my very first best friends. He ministered to David before David and I ever thought about dating, but I think about how cool it is that the Lord used Mike in David's life.*

MUSIC NOTES, CH 15: If you listen closely to the lyrics of some of the Christian Metal bands, you can hear powerful, Word-filled lyrics and worship. I don't claim to understand it all, but I am adding a couple of songs. On the YouTube videos you can listen and read the lyrics.

From the band For Today find *King* on YouTube here: https://youtu.be/RBOXmHcVA6o or in iTunes at: https://music.apple.com/us/album/king/389417916?i=389418767

From the band Sleeping Giant find *Overthrow* on YouTube here: https://youtu.be/NACB8QCAEp8 or in iTunes at: https://music.apple.com/us/album/overthrow/1056426985?i=1056426996

Chapter 17

THE DANGER OF PEDESTALS
AND LIVING ON EITHER SIDE

MOMENTS

Have you ever had a God moment? A moment like when Peter proclaimed Jesus was the Messiah? A moment in perfect communication with Holy Spirit that actually comes through you? A revelation that comes only from above?

Or maybe you've been in the room when a leader, a pastor or someone you trust has spoken such a word and it was such a God moment that it caused holy awe in the room.

If we've ever had the privilege of witnessing such a moment, do we have a tendency to, moving forward, hang on every word that "proceedeth out of that person's mouth" — or worse yet, our own mouth?

I have.

So dangerous. For us and for the person(s) we begin to idolize. Yes, idolize.

IT'S A TRAP!

"It's a trap!" (think your best Admiral Akbar[1] impression.... you know, from Star Wars). Anyway, pedestals can be a trap, whether you have someone lifted high or you find yourself on someone else's pedestal. Either way quite possibly we're not seeing reality. When we have others on pedestals, we often overlook their flaws or we can become so enamored with what we see from a distance, that we don't care about flaws, failures or inconsistencies.

If we find ourselves on someone else's pedestal it can be a slippery-slope, so to speak.

It is impossible for us to live up to others expectations, no matter how hard we try. Occasionally, when realizing we've been placed on a pedestal, even our own flaws can become minimized in our eyes. *We're up there for a reason, right?* That misguided view of ourselves can even seem altruistic; if we hide our flaws from others, we won't let them down.

Either way, when the flaws finally surface, it can be devastating. Whether you're at the base of the pedestal looking up or you're the one living on it.

I've been devastated more than once by looking too closely at my heroes. Likewise, I've devastated others because of the pretend perfection I was wearing.

I faced this pretend perfection one Sunday morning in the middle of devotion time with our worship team. The Lord had been dealing with me during that season of life about being transparent. So rather awkwardly, I was attempting to share a real-life altercation from earlier that morning. I actually don't remember all of the details of the unfortunate event, but I do remember that David and I had words before we left the house for church.

I was furious with him but not for any good reason. Whatever the issue, soon after I realized I was wrong. The Lord had spoken to me that the posture of my heart in that moment was in no condition for leading others into His presence.

So as I'm sharing with the worship team, in the middle of my discourse, one precious woman literally blurted out, "I can't believe it. I can't hear this. I have you on a pedestal. You can't be wrong." Something to that effect. She was serious. I was shocked. Of course it made me feel a little good at first to think someone thought that highly of me... but the more I thought about it, the crazier it became. Surely people don't look at me a certain way because I stand on a stage and sing. Surely they know I am not perfect.

Even as I type this, I see how my need to please others has sometimes fed into the temptation to show pretend perfection. And because I have high expectations for myself, I can tend to expect perfection out of others. Thank God, He always has and continues to use imperfect people. It's the only way that He can use any of us.

THE DANGERS OF LOOKING AT PEDESTALS FROM AFAR

A pedestal is "an architectural support for a column, statue, vase, or the like."[1] It is used to lift up an object so that onlookers can take in the beauty. Doesn't something lifted high in the air draw our attention? The very presence of the pedestal invites us to try and get a glimpse, to admire, perhaps even worship the treasure it holds.

Our culture has pushed us toward pedestals of hero worship for many years. Just pause for a moment to look back at popular culture. We could name names of famous musicians, sports figures, Christians, artists, movie stars, politicians, etc., etc., etc. who we admire. You may be thinking of someone right now. For goodness sakes, there are lists of "The Top 100 Most Famous (insert adverb here)" all over the internet!

It just seems like "we" are always searching for something or someone to "look up to".

It's nothing new. We want someone to follow — just like the Israelites. Remember the golden calf that was forged out of the fire (Exodus 32)? The Israelites wanted something to lead them through the wilderness. The whole reason they asked for it was because Moses was taking too long up on the mountain. They wanted something to follow and they wanted it *now*. There was no being still. No waiting on Moses or on the Lord.

I wonder if that is part of our problem too? We want some *one* or some *thing* to lead us some *where*, now. We're not very patient. We tire quickly of our current place or position. We want to get out of the predicament or situation we find ourselves in. Or we want to do something more, be something more and somehow following someone or something will help us be/do/have more.

> **JESUS & JIMMY CAN FIX ANYTHING**
>
> As I shared in earlier chapters, church was my escape from a trauma-filled home situation. I loved my church. I loved my youth group. I loved Jimmy, my choir director — almost to the point of hero worship.
>
> I remember going to the church office to see him during the day once. In my 13-year-old brain, Jimmy had a direct link to the throne room. His relationship with the Lord seemed bigger than life, so I thought he could fix me. I just didn't know how to ask. I ended up just staring at him. Looking back, it was like seeing a movie star or dignitary that you've admired from afar and wishing for one moment with them. Yet when you're given an audience with that person, you're unable to utter a word. My staring and neediness must have unnerved him. My made-up mentor/mentee relationship was on a shaky foundation at that point, as pedestals of this kind often are.

Think about it... we score if we get "followers" on our social media accounts. If we don't have likes, shares and follows on our postings, we think perhaps there is something wrong with us. Through social media we can view others through filters and lenses and screens and their world's seem perfect.

Social media stars are now called "influencers". So many people hang on the words, actions and endorsements of influencers that companies pay sponsorships for these folks to simply live out their lives in front of others.

> *So don't boast about following a particular human leader.*
> *—1 Corinthians 3:21a*

There is nothing inherently wrong with social media or learning from or being connected to others. The problem arises when we, as individuals, begin looking to any one or any thing other than the Lord as our source. No matter how much knowledge a person has, we are all flawed individuals who need answers ourselves.

WHAT ABOUT SPIRITUAL LEADERS?

Biblically sound preachers and teachers, worship leaders and other spiritual leaders should tell you not to take everything they say as "gospel". After all, The Lord uses people. People. People who have moments, Holy Spirit inspired moments, sometimes moments that are strung together through years of wonderful ministry, praise the Lord! I am grateful for wonderful Bible teachers and I'm privileged to have learned from some of the most integrous people I've ever known.

But people are "peoplie". We stumble. We fail. We get it wrong sometimes. The only way we keep from following someone right off of their pedestal (whether we put them there or not) is to stay in the Word and keep our focus upward on the One we know.

> *"I am the good shepherd; I know my own sheep, and they know me…"*
> *—John 10:14*

Knowing and understanding the Bible is how we know Him. The Word is how we distinguish the voice of God from other voices that vie for our attention, including our own thoughts. The Word is our filter, the lens through which we, as Christians, look at everything. It's how we authenticate what others say. When God is speaking, He will never contradict His Word.

> *"My sheep listen to my voice; I know them, and they follow me."*
> *—John 10:27*

"My sheep listen to my voice … they follow me." Not popular opinion, not the news, not superstar preachers/teachers or even influencers. No one is perfect. Even those we hold in high esteem get it wrong sometimes. While I can learn from others, I must measure every word by the Word. Staying in the Word helps me stay on the path of following Him.

> *Such things were written in the Scriptures long ago to teach us. And the Scriptures give us hope and encouragement as we wait patiently for God's*

> *promises to be fulfilled.* —Romans 15:4

What about words of knowledge? Or prophecies? *What's up with that?* you ask. There are those who have spoken and speak words of knowledge to me. I am grateful for that spiritual gift. Many times the word that is spoken has been a confirmation of something the Lord was already showing me. Even still, I run every word through the Word. The Word of God is my standard. Likewise, any word that I give to someone, I encourage them to seek Him and seek the Word for themselves. Any communication that we perceive the Lord has given us must be able to hold up against the Word — the Sword of Truth.

> *Do not stifle the Holy Spirit. Do not scoff at prophecies, but test everything that is said. Hold on to what is good.* —1 Thessalonians 5:19-21

As Jesus followers, as Christians, as *The Church*, we wholly depend on this vertical relationship we have with Jesus, leaning into Holy Spirit and the Word of God. We don't lean on someone else's understanding or even our own. We search the Word for ourselves, hide it in our hearts, talk about it, ask questions, ask for revelation — but again I say, we can't rely on *every* word that comes out of *any* person's mouth. Only Jesus.

People fall off of their pedestals, sometimes slowly, sometimes all at once. We see it over and over again. We just weren't made to live up there.

What do we do with truths that we have learned from a Bible teacher or preacher or apologist when we suddenly realize they have fallen from grace? Does that discount everything they ever said?

Our hope gets misplaced. Our trust, misguided. Many Christian men and women are raised to superstar status. When they crack under the pressure or morally fail, somehow we're shocked — but again, it's nothing new.

TAKE KING DAVID, FOR INSTANCE

King David had failures, but did the Lord stop using him because he failed? Were the Psalms he wrote thrown out of the canon of Scripture because he failed? We read, quote, write songs from and are often inspired by those very Psalms.

Were God's promises to David canceled because he royally messed up? No! In fact, Jesus is referred to as the Son of David. His wife Bathsheba is one of only 5 women who are mentioned in the lineage of Jesus in the gospel of Matthew. When I understood what that meant, I knew there was hope for me!

I'm thinking of a particular incident in the life King David. (If you haven't read his life story, it is fascinating. You can find the outline of his life and much more in 1 & 2 Samuel and 1 Chronicles.)

God was with David. Remember David and Goliath? That was only the beginning.

The Bible says that David was a man after God's own heart (1 Samuel 13:14, Acts 13:22).

Saul, the previous King of Israel had been removed from office by the Lord, he just didn't vacate the premises. At the same time Saul was removed, the Lord instructed the prophet Samuel to anoint the boy David as King of Israel. For many years David did not sit on the actual throne. David, the boy, grew and God led him in every way, through battle after battle on behalf of Israel. He was becoming so popular that the people of Israel even wrote songs about him, yet he kept his focus on the Lord, listening to His direction.

When David finally came into the kingdom, so to speak, things were going well. He recovered the Ark of the Covenant, making some mistakes along the way, but his heart's motivation was always to please the Lord. David generally learned quickly from his mistakes, turning from then and continuing to seek the Lord — but something changed.

I don't know when it creeped in, but King David's fame seemed to gradually catch up with him. We read in 2 Samuel 8:13:

So David became even more famous...

We begin to see it when one day something unusual happened (2 Samuel 11:1). In this era, kings would normally lead their men into battle every spring. This particular spring, King David sent his men to battle. Without him.

It was during this recess, from high above the city on his rooftop, King David saw a beautiful woman bathing. He sent messengers to find out about her. She was Bathsheba, wife of Uriah, a fact that didn't seem to matter to King David. He was the King and by his next action it seems that the line between what is right and what he wanted didn't even exist.

While Uriah was away, fighting on behalf of the King and all of Israel, King David sent for Bathsheba and had his way with her. Bathsheba became pregnant, so King David devised a plan. He would summons Uriah, her husband home from the war giving Uriah the opportunity to sleep with his wife and no one would be the wiser.

But when Uriah returned, he refused to enjoy the comforts of sleeping in his home with his own wife, because the Ark of the Covenant, which carried the presence of the Lord, and the rest of the army were sleeping in tents on the battlefield. King David tries again the following night, by getting Uriah drunk, but Uriah, loyal to the Lord and to his own mission, slept at the palace entrance.

King David went to the nth degree to cover up the pregnancy and has Uriah killed in battle thinking no one but his right hand man would ever know — but the Lord knew. The Lord told the prophet, Nathan, to confront David in his sin by telling him a story of a great injustice. David, outraged at the injustice, told Nathan that anyone who committed such an act deserves to die. Nathan responded:

> ...You are that man! The Lord, the God of Israel, says: I anointed you king of Israel and saved you from the power of Saul. I gave you your master's house and his wives and the kingdoms of Israel and Judah. And if that had not been enough, I would have given you much, much more. Why, then, have you despised the word of the Lord and done this horrible deed? For you have murdered Uriah the Hittite with the sword of the Ammonites and stolen his wife. —2 Samuel 12:7-9

There's so much more to the story. After Nathan's confrontation King David repents, but his life is never the same. King David was a towering king, literally and figuratively, but he took his eyes off of the Lord. He lowered his vision to what surrounded him. The palace rooftop was elevated, but it wasn't that far off the ground.

The Bible is full of examples of people who made mistakes, had failures, even began to believe their own press — chock full — but if the Lord stopped using any of those people, if he canceled the good that they did before or after their mistakes, there'd be no hope of Him ever using us.

KEEPING IT VERTICAL

I've encapsulated the powerful story of David and Bathsheba in a tiny way, but even as I type this my heart aches because I'm familiar with that tinge of pride that David experienced. I'm reminded of my college days when everything started coming together. I was finally getting to live out everything I wanted — all my dreams coming true. Yet when I took my eyes off of Him and began looking at my surroundings, everything came crashing down.

Isn't that what pride usually does? Seeming so harmless at first, pride begins to be a weight, causing the pedestal to lean heavily to one side, bending towards solid ground... until the pedestal snaps.

Pride cometh before a fall is a familiar saying, based on scripture, "Pride goeth before a fall..." (Proverbs 16:18, James 2:6). The Bible warns us to be aware of pride. If it came on suddenly, we might be able to see it, stopping it before it truly takes root. Instead, it creeps in slowly. Especially when we begin to have some modicum of success.

Most of us have to work at staying humble before the Lord.

My husband, who didn't even know I was writing this chapter, reminded me only a day ago of a something our mentor, David Horton, used to teach us in regards to our musical gifting. Doc used to say, "Never believe your own press. When someone pays you a compliment, just say, 'Thank you,' and move along. Don't take it to heart so much that it gets your head out of shape. The true test of your character isn't struggle — it's success."

Wow.

> *Don't be impressed with your own wisdom. Instead, fear the Lord and turn away from evil. —Proverbs 3:7*

If the ground beneath me begins to elevate and I'm not connected to the Lord, keeping my gaze on Him, pride, among other things, can slowly slither into my thoughts. If I'm not careful, I set myself up for a long, hard trip to the ground.

Conversely, if I allow my gaze to drift, permitting any "high thing" or person to be exalted, whatever that thing is, it is coming between me and Jesus. I have to be careful that my worship belongs only to Him.

Keeping it vertical isn't easy. Over and over we are reminded to look to Him.

Is our attention on Him momentary? Or is it made of amazing moments that encapsulate a life of following Jesus?

MONUMENTAL MOMENTS

We all have Peter moments. Moments of giant faith along with moments of failure. Moments of redemption. Moments of revelation. Holy Spirit reveals truth to us and we speak and it is absolutely anointed, but we are all still human.

I wonder if we, like Peter are supposed to build our "ministry" on moments? Moments of revelation and truth with the Lord is leading us every step of the way. Moments of quiet listening, leaning into the Lord. Moments of giving Him the ALL the glory instead of holding back any part. Moments of connection with Him that display His goodness alone. Moments of vulnerability, allowing His strength to shine through our weakness.

Think about the transfiguration.[2] It was a moment of revelation for Peter, James and John. A priceless glimpse into the realm of heaven. Peter wanted to build a monument right there and put Jesus on this one pedestal for all the world to see, perhaps thinking that by doing so, everyone would surely know that Jesus was the Messiah.

Peter, James and John got to be in on this holy, sacred moment. They beheld a sight no one had ever seen. Jesus was glowing! He was standing right in front of them with Moses and Elijah. The whole experience must have been mind-blowing! Yet Jesus told them it wasn't the moment for the spotlight to be on Him. In that holy, sacred moment, Peter saw one way to lift Jesus up ... but Jesus knew what His platform was to be built on.

> *"And when I am lifted up from the earth, I will draw everyone to myself," Jesus. —John 12:32*

IF I BE LIFTED UP

When Jesus said the verse above to the great throng of worshipers, the celebratory atmosphere on the streets began to change. The crowd understood, through Jewish tradition, that Jesus was saying that He was going to die — yet they couldn't wrap their minds around why. If Jesus was the Messiah, their interpretation of scripture told them He would never die.

Yet Jesus knew what had to be done. He did so while teaching us humility.

> *Though he was God, he did not think of equality with God as something to cling to. Instead, he gave up his divine privileges; he took the humble position of a slave and was born as a human being. When he appeared in human form, he humbled himself in obedience to God and died a criminal's death on a cross. —Philippians 2:6-8*

His wasn't unstable as pedestals often are. The stipe, the vertical beam, was planted in the ground so that it would stay in position. It stood tall for everyone to see. He couldn't fall off of the pedestal He was hoisted upon because nails held Him in place.

> *But many were amazed when they saw him. His face was so disfigured he seemed hardly human, and from his appearance, one would scarcely know he was a man. —Isaiah 52:14*

Purposefully designed, the act of crucifixion was intended for more than death. Death on the Cross was agonizing, excruciating and slow. But even more, the Cross was an instrument of public degradation and shame. Unlike the pedestals we tend to create, the Cross was a platform of complete humiliation.

YET. THIS. IS. THE. PEDESTAL.

This pedestal is not one we are drawn to esteem or admire. Not a popular platform, this pedestal goes against every part of our fleshly being… but this pedestal held the Hope for all people through all the ages.

If we can lift our eyes to see life through this pedestal, our entire worldview changes.

Jesus. Our Redeemer. Our Savior. Our Lord. He was lifted up on this pedestal of shame so that we could have a clear view of heaven. So that we could plainly envision grace.

We can trust Him. We can believe Him. We can lean on Him. We can learn from Him. We can rely on Him. We *can* look up to Him. He will never let us down. He will never fall off of the throne. He will never fail.

> *Turn your eyes upon Jesus*
> *Look full in His wonderful face*
> *And the things of earth will grow strangely dim*
> *In the light of His glory and grace*[3]

My husband sings this chorus often when he leads worship. Lately I am hearing others sing it in new ways in various worship settings. I believe that Holy Spirit is reminding us all to keep it vertical, to fix our gaze on Jesus.

> *We do this by keeping our eyes on Jesus, the champion who initiates and perfects our faith.* —Hebrews 12:2a

HOW DO WE DO IT?

When we learn to fix our eyes on Jesus through every part of our life, we realize He is everything we need. His work on the cross, that pedestal of shame, completed the work He was called to do and gave us a freedom humanity had never before known.

> *Because of the joy awaiting him, he endured the cross, disregarding its shame. Now he is seated in the place of honor beside God's throne.* —Hebrews 12:2b

We can't sit in heavenly places without looking to Jesus. Without seeing Him on the cross. Without understanding His humility. Without dying to our own desires, ambitions or ideology. Without bowing down to fix our gaze on Him.

> *Therefore, God elevated him to the place of highest honor and gave him the name above all other names, that at the name of Jesus every knee should bow, in heaven and on earth and under the earth, and every tongue declare that Jesus Christ is Lord, to the glory of God the Father.*
> *—Philippians 2:9-11*

We don't have to look any further—to any other pedestal. We can be ready to reach the next generation when our gaze is focused on Him. We can be ready for revival. We can be ready for the adventure of our lives when we look to Jesus.

---

[1] *In the movie, as the Alliance mobilize its forces in a concerted effort to destroy the Death Star, Admiral Ackbar encounters an unexpected ambush, which leads him to exclaim, "It's a trap!" Hear it here: https://youtu.be/4F4qzPbcFiA*

[2] *Read about the Transfiguration in Matthew 17:1–8, Mark 9:2–8, Luke 9:28–36 and 2 Peter 1:16-18.*

[3] *Turn your eyes upon Jesus. Songwriter: Lemmel, Helen Howarth (1922). Public Domain*

MUSIC NOTES, CH 17:
Turn Your Eyes from Natalie Grant and Belonging Co. Whew! The new lyrics in the bridge keeps moving us into the new… remember, He is ever doing a new thing! We just have to keep our eyes on Him.

Hear it on YouTube here: https://www.youtube.com/watch?v=61_Ajl10iHE or in iTunes at: https://music.apple.com/us/album/turn-your-eyes-live/1556315862?i=1556315901

Turn Your Eyes. Songwriters: Natalie Grant/Bernie Herms/Andrew Holt/Daniella. © 2020 NG Entertainment/Sony/ATV Tree Publishing / Pure Note Publishing Worldwide (BMI)/ TBCO Publishing (BMI) / Andrew Holt Music Publishing (BMI) / LOVEFUEL PUBLISHING (BMI) (admin at EssentialMusicPublishing.com) All Rights Reserved.

Chapter 18

ABOUT THE BIRDS

PART 3

SLICES OF HEAVEN

One of my friends and prayer partners, Jules, had a vision one evening as she was preparing for prayer. She wasn't asleep, but what she saw was like a dream. When she shared it with me via email, I was gripped by the imagery.

> "I was at prayer Monday night. We hadn't started praying yet but as we were sitting quietly, preparing our hearts, I saw a very detailed vision. It moved by quickly — almost as soon as I saw it, it was gone, but I focused on the details so I could remember.
>
> I saw a girl with blonde hair about 12-to15-years-old. Her hair was to her shoulder blades and pulled back a little bit, with a few strands hanging down the sides of her face. She was in the country, what seemed like a farm. The grass was a beautiful green color and the driveway was gravel and dirt. I saw a hollowed out tractor in the yard where the grass was cut and well manicured. The girl was facing sideways to what I am describing. Behind her to the left and going toward the road was high grass. It looked like wheat but there were also weeds. None of it had been cut or mowed. It was a bright sunny day, no clouds in sky, which was beautiful and very blue.
>
> The area around the farm was wide open and it felt peaceful and secluded. The tractor looked like it was either decoration for the yard or one that didn't run anymore and was hollowed out for play. Behind the tractor was a huge tree with thick, full limbs, pretty green leaves and it hung over the driveway.

The girl was very close to a house. I couldn't see the house but I knew she was close to it because there was a walkway on the side leading towards the house where the grass was worn out and bare. The girl was smiling."

The dream was so appealing! An innocent, young girl playing on a beautiful, secluded farm. The sky was blue, the yard, inviting and the tree was made for climbing. The whole scene was surrounded by flowing wheat fields. It sounded like a slice of heaven.

Yet something bothered me the instant I finished reading the email: the non-functioning tractor coupled with the wheat surrounding the house. Wheat that can't be harvested because the tractor has become a play thing.

Here's the deal — I didn't know anything about farming. What exactly does a tractor do? I looked it up. At its very basic use, a tractor is a vehicle that powers agricultural tasks. For instance, tractors pull farm equipment used for plowing, planting, cultivating, fertilizing, and harvesting crops.

Hmmm.... yet the tractor was out of service — used only for decoration or play while the wheat field remained untouched.

The young blonde girl was so enamored by her beautiful surroundings, she didn't even notice the harvest behind her.

The house? The house couldn't even be seen. It was there, but it wasn't even in the picture. Does that mean it was irrelevant to the scene? Even though the path to it was well worn?

Initially, the vision seemed like a respite — a beautiful, comfortable, innocent sounding place. Secluded — far away from the cares of the world. Certainly a place I'd like to visit. Yet I couldn't help but wonder? Is this a picture of where we are as *The Church*?

Have we become isolated, or worse yet, insulated from the world?

Are we praying for or recognizing the harvest?

Have we become so focused on maintaining what we have that we haven't noticed the harvest that is waiting just outside of the yard?

OUTSIDE OF THE CAGE

Thinking back to "Family Affair" and bird-walking, I ask again — is it possible for us to become comfortable and feel safe inside *The Church*? I say us because I include me. For me, church is a happy place. We hear Good News. We sing. We dance. We worship together and have community. We are fed. We are trained. We learn to operate in the gifts He has given us. We are surrounded by those like us and are often in a place of beauty. Nothing inherently wrong with any of that, but by keeping this wonderful community to ourselves, are we living like Jesus lived?

Jesus went to the Synagogue. He taught in the Synagogue... but His main ministry was in the streets, on the hillsides and in the homes of "sinners".

I write this with tears in my eyes because I too have kept Him to myself too many times.

Are we the "church birds" keeping ourselves separate from the "worldly birds"? Do we truly embrace and live in the freedom Jesus gave us?

Paul says, "... I wrote you in my previous letter asking you not to associate with those who practice sexual immorality. Yet in no way was I referring to avoiding contact with unbelievers who are immoral, or greedy, or swindlers, or those who worship other gods— for that would mean you'd have to isolate yourself from the world entirely!" 1 Corinthians 5:9-10, TPT.

> *...You'd have to isolate yourself from the world entirely!*

Staying inside the church gives us the feeling that we are kept. It's easy to see how being in the cage and being separated from those not like us could be perceived as protection, but our Master doesn't have to keep us locked up to protect us.

He has invited us to live wildly and authentically in the natural habitat He created us for. Within this wild, authentic living, we can reach those who may be trapped in a different cage — those who are truly lost, who don't know the Lord at all.

How can we be co-laborers with Jesus if we don't go out into the fields? I'm not saying that every one of us has to become a missionary to — well, to anywhere. What I am doing is asking more questions. The same questions that helped me consider what it means to be a part of *The Church* versus going to church.

WHAT DOES A WORKER (OR FOR THOSE OF US WHO HAVE BEEN IN THIS A MINUTE, A LABORER) LOOK LIKE?

In prayer one morning, I started reflecting on the harvest. The Lord brought a word picture to my mind. I thought about how crops are harvested and refined in different ways. Coffee beans aren't harvested the same way wheat is harvested or grapes are harvested. Neither is any of it refined or made ready for use in the same way. Coffee beans are processed then dried and milled. Wheat is sifted or separated from what cannot be utilized and then is processed for many different uses. Grapes are harvested to be eaten as fresh produce but are also crushed to make juice and wine.

The laborers for this last day harvest may not look what we "think" they should look like. They are not necessarily going to speak Christianese. They don't care about being famous or having the biggest church. They may attend or even visit church, but they will not be caged in. The Lord is calling these laborers to reach the myriad of different people alive on planet earth.

> *Jesus traveled through all the towns and villages of that area, teaching in the synagogues and announcing the Good News about the Kingdom. And he healed every kind of disease and illness. When he saw the crowds, he had compassion on them because they were confused and helpless, like sheep without a shepherd. He said to his disciples, "The harvest is great, but the workers are few. So pray to the Lord who is in charge of the harvest; ask him to send more workers into his fields."*
> *—Matthew 9: 35-38*

Jesus told the disciples to pray for more workers to be sent into His fields. Does that include us?

Think about Jesus sending out disciples on ministry trips. He told them to go out with basically nothing in hand, no earthly preparation — simply taking what He had given them. In Matthew 10: 9-10 He instructs them, "Don't take any money in your money belts—no gold, silver, or even copper coins. Don't carry a traveler's bag with a change of clothes and sandals or even a walking stick..."

Wow! Talk about living out of our norm. In fact, in the previous verses Jesus tells them, "Heal the sick, raise the dead, cure those with leprosy and cast out demons. Give as freely as you have received." Jesus gave them the opportunity to partner with Him — to take it up a notch in their faith walk — to be in on what He was doing.

Jesus sent them out. Their only qualification? Time with Jesus. They weren't perfect. Each one came from different professions but the unifying factor was Jesus. The Word says they had been healed, delivered or set free by Him and now they were to give back.

Jesus' main ministry was outside of church. He sat on a hillside or in a boat just off shore, in the middle of a town or a village. Any place where people — the outcast, the sinner, the sick — anyone — could come and hear Him. The Bible clearly states that in several locations He healed everyone who was brought before Him. His gifts were and are free and He gave them to people BEFORE they even knew Him. Healing, deliverance, freedom and more were given freely to anyone.

Then He gave the disciples the charge to go out and do what He did.

Am I a disciple? Are you?

His call to you might not look exactly the same as 2,000 years ago, but what if it did?

As we spend time with Him can we, as Jesus commanded, "Heal the sick, raise the dead, cure those with leprosy and cast out demons"? Jesus healed those who asked or were BROUGHT to Him.

When they come asking, can we be ready to fully give them Jesus?

Even after Jesus' resurrection, in Acts 3, Peter and John kept working. When the lame man seated beside the Beautiful Gate asked them for money, he was asking for his need to be met. He probably never dreamed that he could walk again, he was simply trying to exist. The disciples told him that they didn't have money either, but they gave him what they had freely been given — healing through the name of Jesus — and then they helped him up!

This free gift they gave the lame man resulted in 5,000 men who believed in Jesus. Peter and John had no idea the affect their obedience would have on a city. They were focused on one man. When we partner with Jesus through the power of Holy Spirit, He gives us opportunities for a harvest greater than we can imagine.

Jesus met and meets people at their greatest need. Can I do that? Can you?

I'm not throwing stones. In all of my life of ministry I have rarely given up many comforts and have never left my dwelling place without a suitcase in order to go out and reach others. I'm just wondering if I can do more. I'm wondering if I can be more aware of the opportunities He gives me to offer healing, deliverance and rescue in Jesus name. To give people what I have been freely given.

What do you mean, freely given? you ask. In Matthew 10:8 Jesus said, "Give as freely as you have received!" I wonder if that's a part of the problem? I don't even want to type this, but I wonder if some of us "got saved" and never went any further? I wonder if there are some of us who have "fire insurance"[1] but don't understand or live in the fullness of Jesus?

We can't freely give what we don't understand or have not experienced.

DO YOU KNOW A LABORER?

What if we see or know someone who has done what the disciples did — forsaken all to meet other's needs? What about those who have answered His call to freely give? Are we helping them or are we discounting their call? Are we praying for their courage and encouragement to walk it out in obedience? Are we praying for the success of their mission in Jesus?

My friend, Shala, along with her husband and family, picked up their entire world and moved across the country, pursuing a vision for ministry that the Lord gave them. They sold their house, said goodbye to dear friends and to their church family, then left behind everything. Many people, from the outside looking in, thought that perhaps they had missed the mark.

As they were preparing for their journey, Shala and her family had almost all of their belongings stolen. They could have taken that as a sign. They could have said to themselves, *We're not supposed to do this*, but they didn't. In spite of difficulties and challenges and sometimes even a lack of funds, they pursued what God told them to do.

What they thought would happen quickly once they arrived hasn't happened, but what is happening is even greater than they could have imagined.

On a visit back home, Shala shared her heart with me. She told me that the Lord had opened her eyes throughout process. It's different than she had ever imagined. Growing up in church and having been on staff in churches and living quite often in the "expected", this move has taken her out of her comfort zone yet she is learning to embrace her space. She is surrounded by a community of interesting people, people who need to see Jesus, people living in their realness... and she is trying to live her realness in front of them. Through her authenticity, she is able to reach a harvest of people that only God could have prepared for her. She's able to freely give the hope, the life, the joy and the healing that she has received.

There are others. My friend Susan and her husband are missionaries. They have been on furlough for a bit but are now preparing to go back. She can hardly wait. As missionaries, their main ministry is to children, living in and around orphanages, teaching the children and showing them Jesus with skin on. Susan's passion for the children is that they will be able to know, connect with and hear the voice of God for themselves — giving them what she has freely been given — a relationship with Jesus.

Then there's Mindy, who felt led by the Lord to donate a kidney — on behalf of someone she had a "chance" meeting with while ministering to someone else. There's a story we need to tell for sure, but she won't even like my using her name here because to her, she was simply being obedient. How is that being a laborer, you ask? What if the recipient of Mindy's kidney has an opportunity to meet and/or be a co-laborer in the harvest? Is a kidney worth one soul? Mindy would definitely say, "Yes!" The possibilities are endless to those who are obedient.

There's a Christian businessman in my hometown. On any given day you can hear him laughing, making jokes and putting others at ease. Though his manner is boisterous and full of energy, I've witnessed as he quietly gives to further the Kingdom. He doesn't hoard or consume the blessings God has given him. He reinvests those blessings into others whether it's his time, his money, through mentoring or even job opportunities — which once-upon-a-time he gave to me — Tom is a laborer in the harvest.

What can I say about Mama Scar? She is one of my newest friends and while I am still getting to know her, I see her work. She has devoted her life to rescuing women trapped in sex-trafficking. She moves with the Lord, out into the community on dark nights to build relationship, not only with women, but with those who traffic them. She meets them with grace, humility and peanut butter sandwiches, among other things. It is her calling. This work is an extremely, dangerous undertaking that she would never attempt without Yeshua, as she affectionately calls Him. Mama Scar is laboring for souls in a way many of us cannot.

What about Carl? Most days, twice a day, Carl goes to McDonald's. At 85, he is a picture of health. Although he says he gets "a little something to snack on" while he's there, he doesn't go there for the food. Neither does he go to the "nice" McDonald's. He is intentional about his mission, generally driving to "other side of town".

Occasionally he'll go to a Wendy's or even a Big Boy, he explains, if he feels led. The point of his mission: to go to a restaurant where he knows he's more likely to cross paths with people who are down-on-their-luck because most often, they are the ones who will allow him to pray for them at their point of need. Carl's restaurant evangelism opens the door for him to share about a God who saves and changes lives to people who want and need to know this hope.

No matter which place Carl visits, he's simply looking for an opportunity to tell people about Jesus. Jesus changed his life nearly 60 years ago. *Sixty years ago* — yet he can't stop sharing with others the grace he's been freely given.

ON THE ROAD

I was reminded of Philip and the Eunuch[2] (Acts 8:26-40) one Sunday morning as my friend Betty powerfully preached on our relationship with Holy Spirit — truly knowing and understanding who He is and how partnering with Him empowers every part of our lives, including supernatural methods of harvesting.

In this passage in Acts, Philip is instructed to head towards a certain road between Jerusalem and Gaza. The Lord doesn't tell him why but Philip started walking.

As it happened, riding on that road was an Ethiopian eunuch (I'll call him "EE") — a high ranking official under the Queen of Ethiopia. He had traveled to Jerusalem seeking *something*. Most likely he'd heard of the God of Israel and perhaps thought that by going to the temple there he would find answers. However, EE was disappointed in his experience at the temple. Being a eunuch, he would not have been allowed to move beyond the court of the Gentiles. Could he have felt rejected by "the church"? Somehow EE obtained a copy of the book of Isaiah and was reading the scripture aloud as he began the 1,500 mile journey back home.

On the road where he was instructed to walk, Philip noticed the moving carriage. The Lord told him to go and "overtake"[3] or to run alongside the carriage — while it was moving. I don't know about you, but for me I would definitely have to hear from the Lord to attempt running next to a moving vehicle.

Approaching the carriage, Philip heard EE reading aloud and asked him, "Do you understand what you are reading?"

EE said these words:

> "How can I, unless someone instructs me?"
> —Acts 8:31

That Sunday morning this one sentence hit me between the eyes — again. *How can others understand the message of Jesus unless we tell them?*

EE insisted that Philip join him in the carriage. Philip obliged and gave him the message of Jesus, start to finish, leading him to salvation, right there, on the road.

Who knows how long they rode together, but eventually they passed some water and the Ethiopian asked Philip to baptize him. The Bible says that EE went on his way, rejoicing. You'll have to read the passage to see what happened to Philip next.

Who knows the far-reaching impact EE had in Ethiopia as he spread the Good News? I imagine EE rejoicing and telling others that he'd found what he was searching for — the One True Living God.

EE's life was changed forever — on the road.

You can read the whole story in Acts chapter 8 (there's so much more in this chapter) but here's my point: The Lord had already been working, preparing EE's heart. Philip got to harvest this seed because he listened to the voice of the Lord and obeyed, even though what the Lord was asking him to do sounded crazy. *Run alongside a chariot? Seriously, Lord?*

Yet Philip listened and obeyed. He was ready. His passion was to tell anyone who would listen about Jesus, even by supernatural means.

> *For "Everyone who calls on the name of the Lord will be saved." But how can they call on him to save them unless they believe in him? And how can they believe in him if they have never heard about him? And how can they hear about him unless someone tells them? And how will anyone go and tell them without being sent? That is why the Scriptures say, "How beautiful are the feet of messengers who bring good news!"*
> *—Romans 10:13-15*

I want to be like Philip, passionate to tell others about Jesus, hearing and immediately obeying when Holy Spirit speaks to me. I want to move when He says mov, trusting that He already knows the outcome instead of pondering or dissecting the purpose of His direction, trying to foresee the result.

I want to be a laborer in the harvest. I want to be open to God's supernatural ways. I want to have beautiful feet, on the road, ready to move.

GIFTS AND CALLINGS

If you don't yet know Jesus, hang in there with me. For those of us who do, let's remember: We are each given unique gifts. We have life experience. We have experience with Jesus that we can freely give — wherever He gives us the opportunity. Some of us are called to give up what we thought was the good life, in order to live an authentic, fulfilled life, like Shala. Some of us are called to be missionaries in foreign lands, like Susan. Some of us are called to give life, like Mindy. Some, to give hope through our work, like Tom. Some to rescue people from literal darkness, like Mama Scar. Some of us are called to give hope in our own neighborhoods, communities or McDonald's, like Carl.

We all get to live this life empowered by Holy Spirit.

We, *The Church*, are all called to move beyond the walls of a church building — to live authentically and wildly, like Jesus.

[1] *Fire insurance is a "Christianese" term that refers to someone who has only become a Christian as a way of avoiding a terrible hell.*

[2] *Eunuch: noun: 1 a castrated man, especially one formerly employed by rulers in the Middle East and Asia as a harem guard or palace official. https://www.dictionary.com/browse/eunuch*

[3] *Overtake was the word used in the New King James Version of this verse. I love the word picture this presents. "Then the Spirit said to Philip, 'Go near and **overtake** this chariot,'" Acts 8:29, NKJV. The root word in the Greek is, prostrechō, which is a verb translated: to run.*

MUSIC NOTES, CH 18:

The 4HIM song called *The Message* has been in the forefront of my mind since I started writing this book and in particular this chapter. While I love this whole album, this song in particular musically and lyrically drives me to literal tears.

Hear *The Message* on YouTube here: https://youtu.be/Iub2pjTYSXk or in iTunes at: https://music.apple.com/us/album/the-message/304756845?i=304756849

The Message. Songwriters: Mark Harris, Don Koch, Michael Omartian. 1996 Paragon Music Corp. / Point Clear Music/ ASCAP / Definitive Music (admin. by Word, Inc.) Dayspring Music (a div. of Word, Inc.) / BMI / Class Reunion Music / Middle C Music / ASCAP / All rights reserved.

Chapter 19

UPON REFLECTION

And I know that nothing good lives in me, that is, in my sinful nature. I want to do what is right, but I can't. I want to do what is good, but I don't. I don't want to do what is wrong, but I do it anyway. —Romans 7:15, 18-20

I wish that I could say that I have always lived out every principle I write about in this book, but that would not be true.

In one of my favorite passages of scripture, Luke 7:47, Jesus was speaking about the woman who washed His feet. He says: "I tell you, her sins—and they are many—have been forgiven, so she has shown me much love. But a person who is forgiven little shows only little love."

I have been forgiven of sin and fallen short over and over, but there have been moments that I have shown little love. Even to one of my very own.

My baby sister never knew her father. My mom and dad had been divorced for many years and each remarried by the time Amber was born.

I remember that day. I was 19-years old. She actually could have been mine! Diana and I rushed down to the hospital to see her. Amber has been beautiful since birth. A full head of brown hair, dark skin and pretty brown eyes. We were instantly smitten with our baby sister.

I spent a lot of time caring for Am — one of the many pet names I have for her. I remember holding her and praying over her when she was a little baby. At that time, still trapped in my codependency, I felt partially responsible for her because my mom was raising Amber all on her own. I stayed close as much as possible and kept her a lot those first few years. It was never a burden — I so enjoyed spending time with her.

Amber was seven-years-old when David and I got married and moved away. That was a toughie for me, but I knew that it was time. That first summer we were married, my mom asked if Amber could come stay with us for a week or so. As newlyweds we probably should have said no, but I couldn't resist an opportunity to spend time with her.

This pattern — Amber coming to stay with us for all or part of the summer — continued for many years. We had numerous adventures with her, both fun and challenging. We certainly weren't parents... we were barely married! We were newlyweds, still trying to figure out who we were as a couple. I was still trying to work out a lot of my own abandonment issues yet we found ourselves attempting to raise a young lady, part-time.

Every summer we made her a part of our lives, including everything the church had to offer. She accepted Jesus into her heart one summer. I was thrilled.

One fall day, not too long after she had been with us for the summer, Amber called me. She wanted to know how to use the can opener. She was, in her words, trying to make a "substantial snack" after school. I gave her step by step instructions while we talked on the phone and then casually asked, "Where is Mom?"

Amber didn't know that Mom had run an errand and been detained, but she began to unfold her story. She told me how she had walked home from school that day and was locked out of the house. She had a key, but the screen door was locked and she couldn't get in. She was nine. I was 500 miles away and terrified.

So Amber, who is smart and sometimes a smarty-pants, figured out a way to get in. She matter-of-factly told me, "... I remembered that I had scissors in my backpack. So I took out my handy-dandy scissors, cut the screen right by the lock, stuck my fingers in and unlocked the door." Did I mention she was smart and funny?

I relate these few stories so that you can begin to understand our relationship. Over the years Amber has lived with us on multiple occasions. We lived away for all of her formative years, but wherever we were, Mom found a way to get her to us.

PART TIME PARENTING FAILS

When Amber was 13, David and I purchased a promise ring for her. He reluctantly went through with this rite of passage at my insistence, though he didn't feel qualified to do any of it. I just *knew* it was the thing to do in order to keep her from making the same mistakes

I made, so I pushed and pushed until he gave it to her.

I asked my not-quite 30-year-old husband to be a father figure to a teenage girl. So David gave Amber the promise ring that summer while she was with us. When she went back home, she slowly began making some of the same choices I had made as a teenager.

Unfortunately, I did not meet her with the grace that I now urge others to show. A few years later when I found out about Amber's choices, I took the ring away.

I just heard the collective gasp of every reader.

It hurt me to take the ring away, yet it seemed like the only right thing to do. Not only had she had broken the ring, she had broken her end of the deal. Somehow I thought that taking it back would help her see the error of her ways. Upon reflection, I had no idea what I was doing. I hadn't fully thought through my/our end of the bargain. Giving her a promise ring without the right relationship was an easy way out for me.

Upon reflection, I see the absurdity of my thinking.

David and I had been some measure of stability in her life, yet I ripped away that stability with a huge smack of judgment and lack of grace. I can't speak for Amber, but I can't imagine how that conversation affected her. Even now, it makes me sick to think about it.

In recent years I had her purity ring fixed. I gave it back to her, with an apology for how I mishandled that whole incident. She generously forgave me and tells me even now that it's not a big deal, but I see it differently.

If only I had the hindsight then that I have now. If only I had listened to that still, small voice then, instead of hearing the bigger roar of "… her wrongs must be punished…" Oh, God, forgive me again for how I failed at showing grace, especially to someone I love so dearly.

How could I, who had been shown so much grace, not show grace to my baby sister?

I could offer excuses for myself and some of them may even seem valid, but the truth is this: First, it was easier for me try some formula to "keep or protect" instead of setting aside the shame of my past and sharing my mistakes with her. Second, when that attempt failed, instead of grace, I called her guilty and took away my gift of "affection" — rather than getting down in the mess with her to help her figure out what was going on.

Truth.

Amber is so gracious and I am so proud of her. After she read the first drafts of the book, she shared some insights with me and gave me permission to share them with you. "I remember the night you all gave me the ring pretty explicitly — we were at a pizza restaurant in Indianapolis and it meant a lot to me that you had picked out something special for me like that. Other than my engagement ring no one has ever really given me anything significant or symbolic — for basically my entire life. I remember you all chose your birthstone for the ring and that not only was it a purity ring but a promise that the two of you would always be there for me — and you always have been. The hurtful part of your asking for it back wasn't that I had broken the purity promise — it was that you wanted something back that symbolized far more than my virginity to me."

RECONCILIATION & RESTORATION

I'm so grateful that the Lord has restored relationships with other family members. My parents —all three of them (Mom, Dad and Little Mommy) and I have great relationships and we have for many years. God delights in restoration and reconciliation with healthy relationships. That process became so much easier when I let go of what I thought "normal" looked like. We may not look like other families, but we love one another and cherish opportunities to spend time together. In fact, many Thanksgiving dinners we spend with ALL of our family — including the three of them!

One of the greatest joys in my life has been reconnecting with my brother, Shawn. I love spending time with him and his wife, Danielle and my two baby-kids (that's what I call them), Corinne and Greyson. We are family.

During much of Shawn's formative years I lived away and while occasionally Dad would bring him to see us on a trip, it was never for very long. I missed out on so much.

I can't describe to you the immense feelings of love, joy and contentment I feel when the words roll of my tongue, "My brother." It's like the connection with him that I longed for is finally made, forever.

David will ask, "Who are you texting with?"

I say, "My brother."

Someone will ask, "What did you do last night?"

"We went to dinner with my brother."

It might sound silly to you, but for many years I felt separated from him. He had a life that I knew nothing about. He lived with his mother and because my relationship with her was rocky, I didn't cross the lines to make sure I connected with him.

I had such guilt and regret about that. It was hard to overcome because I felt like such a failure.

But God has a way of restoring the years.

My brother. I only have one. I am so proud of him. Maybe too proud sometimes... LOL... He is a police officer, now a detective in a nearby city. One day, he got recognition for his work that was featured on a local news station video. Being a big sis who missed most of his childhood, I carefully took a screenshot and edited it, drawing a heart around my brother! Then I posted and boasted about him on Facebook, tagging him in the post. Shortly after that I found out that he received much ridicule over that post from his Brothers-In-Arms... sorry, Bubs, but I was and am so proud of you!

God always, always, always wants reconciliation. (See 2 Corinthians 5: 18-21.)

Most of us can look back at the craziness of our own lives and analyze it to death, but the question remains: Are we giving grace in the same measure that we have been shown the grace of Jesus?

Are we loving like Jesus loves? Willing to get down in the complicated lives of others, including our loved ones, to help them sort through their brokenness? Making sure they understand the love of a Savior who loves them without conditions?

Jesus said, "So now I am giving you a new commandment: Love each other. Just as I have loved you, you should love each other, " John 13:34. I fail at this often, but His grace is sufficient.

I still need His grace, daily. I thank God for new mercies every morning because when I begin to lose sight of Jesus, of His grace and my lack of thereof, my worldview narrows.

SCARS, BEGINNINGS & ENDINGS

The Church walked with me while I was searching — when my "normal" had thrown life at me in such a way that I wasn't sure who I was. I had unhealthy relationships with men and women in both physical and emotional ways. I thought I was the one who was supposed to take on everyone else's stuff and make it better. And if those that were *The Church* in my life would have left me in my searching, I could still be lost.

Even after I was solid in my relationship with Jesus, I still needed to grow in grace. I thought that I needed to live in "the opposite" — opposite of who I was before Jesus. I had many moments of misjudgment and missed opportunities to be *The Church*. Many, too many days when my attitude was .... religious.

I wish that I could tell you that everything about my life has been full of fairytale endings. I wish that I could tell you that shame and the regret of my past never tried to haunt me or make me feel unworthy.

That would be untrue. But God.

> *But God still loved us with such great love. He is so rich in compassion and mercy.* —Ephesians 2:4 TPT

I can tell you this: the acute pain from the memories of my past is gone. Rarely do I experience intense pain when I reflect on certain incidents or my old feelings of abandonment and shame. Early in the process, there were moments of pain that were so strong, the painful feeling radiated down my arms and into my hands — my body literally ached. Intensely painful moments that I remember very well.

But the great love of God changed everything and He used people to make an impact on me. People who make up — *The Church*.

When I look at the past I only see the scars. Every major wound results in some degree of scarring. Even Jesus has scars. He offered His scars to the disciples as proof that it really was Him. In John 20:27 Jesus invited Thomas to, "Put your finger here, and look at my hands. Put your hand into the wound in my side."

Maybe my scars prove that I'm really me. God never wastes one ounce of our pain — it's just that sometimes we don't want to be in touch with that pain. If I hide my scars or pretend the injuries never happened, am I being authentic?

MUSIC NOTES, CH 17:

Too Many Times from Michael W. Smith's first project, aptly titled *Project*. I wanted to open the chapter with a specific lyric from this song, but I opted to use the verse from Paul as I believe this verse sums up a place we all wrestle in. Michael and his wife Debbie wrote this song which is lyrically both raw and real. One of my favorite songs from one of my favorite albums, from one of my favorite people(s).(And yes, I actually did meet him back in my Berean days.)

Hear it on YouTube here: https://www.youtube.com/watch?v=60IbExoTdC8 or in iTunes at: https://music.apple.com/us/album/too-many-times/359221883?i=359221928

Too Many times. Songwriters: Debbie Smith / Michael W. Smith. Copyright © 1983 Reunion Records.

Chapter 20

SILVERWARE REFLECTIONS

For me, the whole point of this writing is about being obedient, sharing with others where I've been, how I made it (and continue to make it) and asking church-goers, both current and former, to see with fresh eyes — renewed vision. It's about asking brothers and sisters in Christ to check themselves against the Word. It's about finding out His heart and passionately following where He leads.

My relationship with the church was not always the best relationship I have ever had, but as I've been working through my story there is this recurring entity, a great miracle, called *The Church*. Jesus keeps giving me glimpses of His spotless bride. His patience, kindness and teaching have given me a vision of *The Church* that He has called us to be.

Not a building — people. Not a judge's chambers — mercy. Not a place to run from, but a place to run to — a place to be embraced. Not what we think it should look like, but streams in the desert (Isaiah 43:19).

What if we, as *The Church*, begin to move out into our communities?

The Lord continues to speak to me when I open my silverware drawers. Remember the pieces of my original silverware that I thought were lost? What if they are serving somewhere else? What if they are serving in the community at large?

Are we a part of the body that resembles an active, working silverware drawer? Or are we set aside, rarely used, waiting to be polished? Too good or too fancy to be put into everyday service?

I was definitely a rusty serving spoon yet the Lord didn't set me aside. He continues to polish me, continues to use me in unique ways. *The Church* has been a part of that preparation.

God designed each of us uniquely. Looking at my silverware drawer reconfirms this truth for me. I wish that each piece of silverware in my drawers was different in order to reflect this truth we are "... fearfully and wonderfully made." Made uniquely, but designed to work together.

Just like my silverware drawer has many different pieces, we the church are made up of many different people. Literally, I now have 55 spoons and over half of them are different. Spoons were created with the same function in mind, but they differ in look and the way they approach serving. Some spoons have deep bowls. Some have wider necks, some have longer handles, some are ladles, some are slotted. Still, they all have one purpose — moving food. Yet they look, feel and do what they do, differently.

How much difference can one person — or serving spoon — really make? Could it be that we feel unnecessary because someone is already doing what we are called to do? I've even said it to myself, *someone else is doing that — they don't need me*. Sometimes we listen to the thoughts that tell us, "The job is too big or the cost is too great or the little things that I can do won't matter.

But the little things do matter. The most important thing we can do is hear what Jesus is speaking — to each of us.

STAYING TUNED IN

Are we willing to lay aside what we think we know, even what we perceive in order to make sure we are hearing His voice? We have been given the amazing privilege to reach, disciple and love the way Jesus loves.

One small act of obedience to His voice could help change the trajectory of a life.

The beautiful thing is this: We don't have to save the whole world, in fact, we don't even save one. That is ALL Jesus. Yet we get to be in on what He's doing because He chooses to use us.

Our privilege is to stay in tune with Him, seizing the opportunities He sets before us to bring others to Him. He does the rest.

My Son and The Sweetness, as I call my daughter-in-law, Ashley, had a dog named Charlie. Devin, Ashley and a friend used to take their dogs to the park almost every day for exercise. One day we accompanied them and watched as they used this contraption to throw a whiffle ball high and far into the distance. It was so high that the dogs could not see the ball, yet they heard it whistle as it spun through the air. With great precision, the dogs actually met the ball when it hit the ground and then, they brought it back their master.

The dogs were tuned-in to that sound they heard because it came from their Master's hand. They carried their treasure back to Him. The Master took care of the rest.

We, *The Church*, have an opportunity in this moment to tune in to what Holy Spirit is saying.

Yes, His church does exist today. We are *The Church*. We are awakening. We are alive and we are preparing for a great Harvest.

> *The church, you see, is not peripheral to the world; the world is peripheral to the church. The church is Christ's body, in which he speaks and acts, by which he fills everything with his presence.*
> *—Ephesians 1:23 MSG*

Chapter 21

FOOD FOR THOUGHT

I want you to show love, not offer sacrifices. I want you to know me more than I want burnt offerings. —Hosea 6:6

HEALTHY THINGS GROW

If you've been around church for even a moment, it is likely that you are familiar with or maybe even learned the basic plan of salvation. Perhaps you even stated your confession that Jesus is Lord — but is He really the Lord of your life?

Have you been rescued by Him? Do you realize your need for a savior, still? Even after being "saved" for 5, 10, 25 or 50 years?

Asking questions is one of the ways I look introspectively and how we have journeyed through this book together so please bear with me as I ask just a few more.

Have you been changed?

If we haven't been changed, do we really know Him? Do we attend church or participate in a church because it is expected? Or maybe because our family has always done so?

Do we think that being, doing, living "good" is enough? I recently read *A Change of Affection* by Becket Cook. (I've never met him, but I love him. He's my people.) His life story gripped me in a way that no other story has in a long time. When he met Jesus his life completely changed. He did a 180 — just like Paul. He walked away from everything — *everything* to follow Jesus.

Was it that way with you? For me it was a process. Even in the process we can have wonderful moments of progress. Are you making progress?

Are you intentionally and deliberately an apprentice of Jesus? Is He your story?

Are you hiding the Word in your Heart? Soaking in His presence? Making Him your life's song?

Are you "all in"?

P.G. says quite often, "Healthy things grow." How are you growing in the Lord?

Do my questions leave you with questions? Do they make you uncomfortable, like they made me? At the beginning of this journey I found myself wondering, *what I have been doing while going to church for so many years?*

> *That is why the Lord says, "Turn to me now, while there is time. Give me your hearts. Come with fasting, weeping, and mourning. Don't tear your clothing in your grief, but tear your hearts instead."*
> *—Joel 2:12-13a*

Journey with me. I dare you. One of my prayers has been, Lord, help me be able to sit with You in the uncomfortable. It's hard!

If you dare, take my challenge. Sit in the uncomfortable. Invite Holy Spirit to help you sift through your relationship with Jesus and *The Church*.

> *Return to the Lord your God, for he is merciful and compassionate, slow to get angry and filled with unfailing love. He is eager to relent and not punish. —Joel 2:13b*

PRAYER

Jesus, You died for all. Once for all. You changed everything. Help us to be so intimately acquainted with Your Word that it pours out of us. Help us to keep our guard up and not be deceived by anything that is not like You. We want to speak the Truth in LOVE so that blinded eyes are opened.

Awaken us, Your people, I pray.

www.ingramcontent.com/pod-product-compliance
Lightning Source LLC
Chambersburg PA
CBHW072014070526
44583CB00015B/1483